6

D0291178

~

Saints of the
American Wilderness

John A. O'Brien

Saints of the American Wilderness

The Brave Lives and Holy Deaths
of the Eight North American Martyrs

SOPHIA INSTITUTE PRESS®
Manchester, New Hampshire

Saints of the American Wilderness was formerly published as *The American Martyrs* in 1953 by Appleton-Century-Crofts, Inc., New York. This 2004 edition by Sophia Institute Press® contains minor editorial revisions to the original text.

Sophia Institute Press®
Box 5284, Manchester, NH 03108
1-800-888-9344
www.sophiainstitute.com

Nihil obstat: Very Rev. T. E. Dillon, Censor Librorum
Imprimatur: John Francis Noll, D.D., Bishop of Fort Wayne

Library of Congress Cataloging-in-Publication Data

O'Brien, John A. (John Anthony), 1893-1980.
    Saints of the American wilderness : the brave lives and holy deaths of the eight North American martyrs / John A. O'Brien.
        p. cm.
    Rev. ed. of: The American martyrs. 1953.
    Includes bibliographical references (p.).
    ISBN 1-928832-90-3 (pbk. : alk. paper)
    1. Jesuits — New France — Biography. 2. Christian martyrs —
New France — Biography. 3. Jesuits — Missions — New France —
History — 17th century. 4. Wyandot Indians — Missions — New
France — History — 17th century. 5. Indians of North America—
Missions — New France — History — 17th century. I. O'Brien,
John A. (John Anthony), 1893-1980. American martyrs. II. Title.
BX3755.O27 2004
272'.9'09713 — dc22   2004012183

Contents

Introduction. vii

〜 Book One
The Curtain Rises 3

〜 Book Two
Isaac Jogues
René Goupil
Jean de Lalande. 19

〜 Book Three
Jean de Brébeuf
Gabriel Lalemant. 91

〜 Book Four
Antoine Daniel 171

〜 Book Five
Charles Garnier
Noël Chabanel 197

〜 Book Six
The Curtain Falls 239

Bibliography 251

~

Introduction

The chief sources of our knowledge of the life, customs, and languages of the Indians, and of the works and lives of the missionaries, colonists, traders, and others who entered upon the stage of New France from 1610 to 1672, are the letters and reports that the Jesuit missionaries sent to their superiors in France and Rome.

These letters and reports were published in a series of seventy-three volumes under the title *The Jesuit Relations and Allied Documents*, which have won unstinted praise from scholars throughout the world as a monumental contribution to American historical scholarship.

The writers were highly educated men, acute observers, conscientious recorders of what they saw and did. Leaving the most civilized country in Europe, these Frenchmen plunged into the unknown American wilderness and came face-to-face with the American Indian, whom they often found to be of the utmost ferocity.

To achieve the spiritual conquest of the Indian, in all his various nations, tribes, and dialects, the missionaries had first to attain thorough knowledge of his languages, customs, and ceremonies, to

Saints of the American Wilderness

penetrate into his strange cults, and to secure insight into his habits of thought and action. The missionaries were the first students of the American Indian, and they had the best possible opportunity for pursuing their study, since they lived in his wigwams and traveled with him on long journeys through the wilderness and upon the myriad lakes and rivers.

The missionaries had attended the best colleges and universities in France. They were versed in the sacred sciences and in many branches of secular knowledge. They were able to make astronomical and meteorological observations, to chart maps, and to note what was peculiar in forestry, vegetation, and animal life. They were shrewd observers of racial characteristics, and one of them, Joseph François Lafitau, is recognized as the founder of modern technology.

They studied the Indian languages as missionaries eager to converse in them, and as philologists. Brébeuf's pioneer studies of the Huron and Petun languages laid the foundation for most subsequent work in these tongues. And Pierre Potier's seven books on the Huron language have proved so valuable that the Ontario government published them in 1920 at public expense.

Many of the missionaries' letters were written in Indian huts and wigwams and at campfires, amid a chaos of distractions: dogs barking, mosquitoes swarming over face and hands, smoke covering the missionaries like a pall, and dogs and children crawling over them alternately. Frequently the writers were suffering from fatigue and hunger, from sickness, or from wounds inflicted by rude hosts who, at the twinkling of an eye, could change into jailers and tormentors upon the whisper of a medicine man or sorcerer.

The style of the letters is nearly always simple and direct, informal and factual. The narrators indulge in no self-glorification or self-pity; they do not dwell needlessly upon the details of their own hardships, but rather set forth the facts with candor and objectivity.

With these letters begins the written history of the north: the valleys of the St. Lawrence, the Great Lakes, and the Mississippi. A few of the French traders — the *coureurs de bois* — had preceded the missionaries in some solitary places, but they seldom made records. Yet, when they came to the chapels to receive the sacraments after their long roaming, they would impart to the missionaries their experiences, which were reflected in the letters to France.

Considering the difficulties, it is a wonder that anything at all was written and dispatched. Jogues wrote some of his letters with a hand on which there remained but one whole finger; blood from a wound stained the paper. Gunpowder was his ink; the earth, his table. Many of the Indians regarded writing as magic and feared that it might do harm to them. Chaumonot, one of the chroniclers, at times had to write in secluded places and carry his letters in his clothing, because of the superstitious fear with which the Indians sometimes regarded them.

The missionaries' accounts of life in the wilderness have the thrill of excitement, the romance that comes of the struggle for enormous stakes, and the deep human interest of truthful narrative. The American historian Francis Parkman could scarcely lay down a volume of the *Relations,* once he had taken it up. "They appeal," he remarks, "equally to the spirit of religion and the spirit of romantic adventure. . . . They hold a high place as authentic and trustworthy documents."[1]

George Bancroft writes, "The history of the Jesuit Mission is connected with the origin of every celebrated town in the annals

[1] Francis Parkman, *The Jesuits in North America* (Boston: Little, Brown and Co., 1867), vi.

of French America. Not a cape was turned, not a river entered, but a Jesuit led the way."[2]

When the letters that constituted the *Relations* were published in France, they stirred up enormous interest. They inspired the support of people, king, and aristocracy and encouraged many thousands of adventurous immigrants to cast their lot with the New World. Hence, the *Relations* not only record the history of New France, but they also had much to do with the making of that history.

The present volume incorporates the results of modern historical research, but the story it tells will be essentially the same as told by the missionary pioneers themselves in their letters from Indian campfire, wigwam, and canoe. It will capture the highlights of the seventy-three volumes of *The Jesuit Relations and Allied Documents*.

Playing the central roles in the powerful missionary drama of New France were eight Jesuits who died as martyrs for the Christian Faith. They were the first in North America to be canonized as saints by the Catholic Church. Six of the eight were priests: Isaac Jogues, Jean de Brébeuf, Gabriel Lalemant, Antoine Daniel, Charles Garnier, and Noël Chabanel; two were lay assistants: René Goupil and Jean Lalande. The eight are commonly known as the Jesuit Martyrs of North America.

This volume tells the story of their adventures, their apostolic labors among the Indians, and their heroic deaths at the hands of those to whose evangelization they had dedicated their lives. Their story is, in miniature, the story of the whole missionary enterprise of the first half of the seventeenth century, an undertaking

---

[2] George Bancroft, *History of the United States* (Boston, 1850), Vol. 3, 122.

that sought to win for Christianity and for civilization the whole Indian population of New France and ultimately of all North America.

There were many other missionaries, of the Society of Jesus and other orders. Their dedication to the work of conversion was heroic, ending often in martyrdom. They, too, endured hardship and suffering with patience and even with joy. They have a just claim upon our esteem and gratitude. It is with no disparagement of their magnificent achievements that we confine our story largely to the eight canonized Jesuits, who shall stand as the symbols of all the North American missionaries. In honoring these, we honor all.

The amount of historical data on the eight martyrs varies greatly. Accordingly, the treatment of the eight will differ in length and detail. With Jogues and Brébeuf, the source material is fairly abundant; with Goupil and Lalande, exceedingly meager, and their labors will have to be etched in with the larger portrait of Jogues, whose humble assistants they were.

The eight carried on their work during approximately the same time, often in the same localities, and sometimes together. In treating them and their careers singly, therefore, we have not been able to avoid occasional overlapping of incidents.

~

Saints of the
American Wilderness

Book One

The Curtain Rises

~

Chapter 1

The Jesuits had come to a territory larger than all France. Roughly, it stretched from the Atlantic Ocean west to Lake Superior and the Mississippi; south from Hudson Bay to Lake Erie. This was New France. The missionaries penetrated even beyond these frontiers in their quest of souls, and they regarded all of the New World as the legitimate field of their apostolate, but their labors were concentrated in the territory of New France.

This comprised the areas now known as Nova Scotia, Cape Breton and Prince Edward islands, New Brunswick, the great provinces of Quebec and Ontario, and the states of Maine and New York. The broad highway through the wilderness was the St. Lawrence and its tributaries. The fortified settlements at Quebec and Montreal constituted the slender and precarious beachhead the French had established in the American forest.

The missionary center from which the Jesuits radiated out to their scattered missions among the Hurons was Fort Sainte Marie. This was on the east bank of a mile-long stream that connects Lake Isiaragui with Georgian Bay; Georgian Bay opens westward into Lake Huron. The site of Fort Sainte Marie is today marked by the Martyrs' Shrine, to which come pilgrims to honor the eight Jesuit Martyrs of North America. It is near the present town of Midland, at the south end of Georgian Bay, in the heart of what was once Huronia, the kingdom of the Hurons.

The vast expanse of the American wilderness had been brought to the attention of the French by a number of voyages of discovery. John Cabot, sailing from Bristol, reached the shores of Canada in 1497. Soon afterward, fishermen from Europe steered their vessels along the Newfoundland Banks and the coasts of North America. In 1534 a French expedition under Jacques Cartier sailed from St. Malo and entered the gulf that he named after St. Lawrence.

The following year, Cartier pushed up the gulf until it narrowed into a river. As his ship neared a towering promontory, the pilot exclaimed in his Norman dialect, *"Que bec!"* ("What a beak!"), thus giving Quebec its name. Planting the banner and cross, Cartier proclaimed Francis I as king of all this territory and its inhabitants.

Cartier ventured farther up the river. He reached an island dominated by a cone-shaped mountain and gave to it the name Mont-Real ("Royal Mountain"). On his return to France, however, Cartier brought back no cargo of precious metals and jewels, nor had he found the long-sought western route to India, and his new world was largely forgotten. Not until seventy years had passed were sustained efforts made to confirm the claims of Cartier.

In 1603 Samuel de Champlain sailed up the St. Lawrence. The following year he was at the Bay of Fundy, where he had a share in founding the first French colony in North America: Port Royal, now Annapolis Royal, in Nova Scotia. In 1608 Champlain established the Quebec settlement. A fervent Christian, who wished to spread the Christian Faith among the Indians, he enlisted the aid of the Franciscan Récollet fathers. It was the Récollets who inaugurated the seventeenth-century missions in interior Canada.

From 1608 until his death in 1635, Champlain worked unceasingly to develop Canada as a colony, to promote the fur trade, to
explore the interior, and to evangelize the Indians. He sailed
southward from the St. Lawrence and came upon the beautiful
lake that bears his name. He pushed westward and then up the St.
Lawrence and Ottawa rivers in hopes of reaching China. He came
to what seemed inland seas — Lake Huron and Lake Ontario —
but did not penetrate to the lakes that stretched even farther west.

This was the era of the Thirty Years War (1618-1648), and during that great upheaval, England was often in conflict with France.
Indeed, as early as 1613, the English from Virginia had almost
completely wiped out the French settlement at Port Royal, and
when in 1629 a small English fleet appeared suddenly at Quebec,
Champlain was forced to surrender.

Three years later, however, Canada was restored to France by
the treaty of St. Germain-en-Laye. Under the aegis of Cardinal
Richelieu, "The Company of New France," popularly known as
"The Company of One Hundred Associates," was formed. To it was
granted the whole St. Lawrence valley, and for fifteen years, dating
from 1629, it enjoyed a complete monopoly of trade. Products from
its territory entered France free of duty. In return for these privi-
leges, the Company was to transport three hundred colonists a
year to New France, and for each settlement it was to provide three
priests. The Company virtually controlled New France until 1663.

England, France, and the Netherlands looked with greedy eyes
upon the New World. Instead of pooling their resources to help all
the colonists in their desperate struggles against the elements, the
wilderness, and the Indians, the three European powers thwarted
one another's colonizing efforts whenever possible. Paralleling, on
a lesser scale, the activities of the English, who had come all the
way from Virginia to wipe out the French settlement at Port

Royal, were the tactics of the Dutch at New Amsterdam and Rensselaerswyck on the Hudson, who pitted the fierce Iroquois against the French, arming their Indian allies with muskets.

Through its colonists, each of the European powers sought to gain the upper hand in the New World and to secure either a monopoly or at least a lion's share of the Indian fur trade. There was frequent friction among the colonists and among their copper-skinned allies.

The Indian population Cartier had found in Montreal and Quebec in 1535 had vanished by the opening of the next century. In its stead was another race, widely different in language and customs. In the region that is now New York State, the Iroquois were rising to a ferocious vitality. Only the presence of Europeans prevented them from subjecting, absorbing, or exterminating all other Indian communities east of the Mississippi and north of the Ohio.

Two great families of tribes, distinguished by a radical difference of language, occupied the vast wilderness from the Mississippi to the Atlantic, from the Carolinas to Hudson Bay. These were the Algonquins and the Iroquois.

Extending over parts of Virginia and of Pennsylvania, over New Jersey, southeastern New York, New England, New Brunswick, Nova Scotia, and lower Canada were the tribes speaking various Algonquin languages and dialects. They stretched, moreover, along the shores of the Upper Lakes and into the dreary northern wastes beyond. They roved throughout Wisconsin, Michigan, Illinois, and Indiana, and detached bands ranged the lonely hunting grounds of Kentucky.

Like a great island in the midst of the Algonquins lay the tribes who spoke the generic tongue of the Iroquois. The true Iroquois, or Five Nations, were in central New York, from the Hudson to the Genesee. The "five nations" were the Mohawks, the Oneidas, the Onondagas, the Cayugas, and the Senecas. To these were added a sixth tribe, the cognate Tuscaroras from North Carolina, after the war of 1711-1712.

Southward of the Five Nations, on and near the Susquehanna, were the Andastes, also speaking an Iroquois tongue; westward, the Eries, along the southern shore of Lake Erie, and the Neutral nation, along the northern shore of Lake Erie from Niagara toward the Detroit River. The settlements of the Hurons lay near the lake to which they have left their name.

The densest of the Algonquin populations, despite a recent epidemic that had wiped out thousands, was to be found in New England. Here were the Mohicans, the Pequots, the Narragansetts, the Wampanoags, the Massachusetts, and the Penacooks — all of them thorns in the side of the Puritans. For the most part, these tribes were favorable specimens of the Algonquin stock. They tilled the soil and were thus, to a certain extent, spared the extremes of misery and degradation to which the nomadic hunter tribes were frequently reduced. They were apt fishermen and tended toward the coast; here, before the epidemic, Champlain and Captain John Smith had observed many settlements, studded with wigwams and waving with harvests of maize.

The Algonquins were driven eastward by the Iroquois with relentless hostility. Some of the tribes paid annual tribute to the tyrant, while others fled in terror at the sound of the Mohawk war cry. In the western parts of New England, the population was thinning rapidly; in the north, it soon disappeared. Indeed, northern New Hampshire, the whole of Vermont, and western Massachusetts had no human tenants except the roving hunter or prowling warrior. Although this group of Algonquin tribes was relatively populous, it is doubtful, had union been possible, whether all of them united could have mustered eight thousand warriors.

Well to the north, on the Ottawa River, the silence of the wilderness was broken only by the splash of the paddle; but beyond, still further north, was the small Algonquin band called *La Petite Nation* ("The Little Nation"), together with one or two other feeble communities. They pitched their tents far from the banks, through fear of the ubiquitous Iroquois. Not nearer than three hundred miles along the winding Ottawa was there to be found another Algonquin tribe, *La Nation de l'Isle* ("The Island Nation"), which occupied the great Island of the Allumettes.

To the southwest, many days' travel through the trackless wilderness, lived a people speaking an Iroquois dialect. The change from the famished wanderers of the Saguenay was considerable. Here were populous towns, rude fortifications, and ripening harvests. These were the Hurons, of whom the modern Wyandots are a remnant. They were the people upon whom the Jesuit missionaries concentrated their chief efforts to convert and civilize.

The territory occupied by the Hurons is now the northern and eastern portion of Simcoe County, Ontario, and comprises the peninsula formed on the west by Nottawasaga and Matchedash bays, adjoining Georgian Bay (off Lake Huron) and the Lake Simcoe and the River Severn on the east. A census taken by Father Brébeuf in 1636 showed a total population of about thirty thousand.

The domain of the Hurons was an alternation of meadows and deep forests, interlaced with footpaths leading from town to town. Although some of these settlements were fortified, most were open and defenseless. The dwellings clustered, with little semblance of order, over an area ranging from one to ten acres. They were of a construction peculiar to all tribes of Iroquois lineage, averaging about thirty-five feet in length, breadth, and height. In some villages there were dwellings, or longhouses, up to two hundred forty feet long. The frame of a longhouse consisted of tall, strong saplings planted in a double row and bent till they met at the top, where they were tied together. Other saplings were planted at the ends of the dwelling. Large sheets of bark covered the entire frame, except at the crown of the arch, where, along the full length of the house, a foot-wide opening was left for admission of light and escape of smoke. Upon the bark covering, split poles were made fast with cords of linden bark.

Down the middle of the house were the fires; around each of them slept two families clustered closely together, their dogs lying pell-mell among them. Despite the opening along the crown of the roof, the walls were usually thick with soot from the fires, for there was no proper draft, nor windows to carry away the smoke. So pungent was the atmosphere that it produced regular inflammation of the eyes and often blindness in old age.

Fleas and vermin abounded as the result of unsanitary practices, and the entire abode was usually permeated with an acrid stench. Sometimes more than twenty families, without even a pretense at privacy, lodged in the single chamber that constituted the dwelling.

"He who entered on a winter night," observes Parkman, "beheld a strange spectacle: the vista of fires lighting the smoky concave; the bronzed groups encircling each — cooking, eating, gambling, or amusing themselves with idle badinage; shriveled hags, hideous with threescore years of hardship; grisly old warriors, scarred with Iroquois war clubs; young aspirants, whose honors were yet to be won; damsels gay with ochre and wampum; restless children pell-mell with restless dogs. Now a tongue of resinous flame painted each wild feature in vivid light; now the fitful gleam expired, and the group vanished from sight, as their nation has vanished from history."[3]

---

[3] Parkman, *The Jesuits in North America*, xxvii.

Although there was no individual ownership of land among the Hurons, each family had exclusive right to as much as it saw fit to cultivate. Working with hoes of wood and bone, the squaws sowed the corn, beans, pumpkins, tobacco, sunflowers, and Huron hemp. They used no manure, and at intervals of ten to thirty years, when soil was exhausted and firewood distant, the settlement was abandoned and a new one built. The staple food was Indian corn, cooked without salt in a variety of forms, each more insipid than the last. Dog flesh was held in high esteem, and venison was a luxury found only at feasts. The Hurons were less improvident than the roving Algonquins, and stores of provisions, chiefly corn, were laid up against a season of want.

Female life among the Hurons was marked in youth by license and in age by drudgery. Marriage existed and polygamy was exceptional, but divorce took place at the whim of either party. The Hurons were notoriously dissolute, far more so than the wandering and starving Algonquins.

In March and April the squaws gathered the year's supply of firewood, then busied themselves with sowing, tilling, harvesting, smoking fish, dressing skins, making cordage and clothing, and preparing food. "Their women," said Champlain, "are their mules." The old women, hideous and despised, often exceeded the men in cruelty and vindictiveness.

To the braves fell the tasks of building houses, making weapons, pipes, and canoes, and hunting and fishing. Summer and autumn were their seasons to make war, hunt, fish, and trade. Their domestic life was for the most part one of leisure and amusement, in which gambling, feasting, smoking, and dancing bulked large. They were desperate gamblers and sometimes staked their all — ornaments, clothing, canoes, pipes, weapons, and wives — in their games of chance.

Among these members of the Iroquois family, sickness was deemed the result of sorcery, demonic spirits, or some other super-natural influence. Their medicine man was a conjuror, and his remedies were preposterous, often revolting. He would beat, shake, and pinch his patient; howl, yell, and rattle a tortoise shell at his ear to drive out the evil spirit. He would bite him until the blood flowed and then display a piece of wood, bone, or iron which he had concealed in his mouth and affirmed to be the source of the disease, now happily removed.

The Huron nation, a confederacy of four distinct, contiguous Iroquois tribes, was increased to five by the addition of the Tionon-tates. It was divided into clans and governed by chiefs whose office was hereditary through the female. There were two principal chiefs: one for peace, one for war. In addition, there were other chiefs assigned to special national functions, such as the directing of trading voyages to other nations and the directing of the great feast of the dead.

Each nation of the confederacy had its own separate organiza-tion, but at certain periods grand councils of the united nations were held, which were attended not only by the chiefs, but by a great concourse of the people also. At all councils, the chiefs and principal men voted on proposals by means of small sticks or reeds, the voice of the plurality prevailing.

Although the Hurons belonged to the broad family of Iroquois, they were attacked by no nation so ferociously and incessantly as by the main Iroquois nation; and in the story of the Jesuit missions they will be treated quite distinctly from the parent family.

As we have said earlier, the Iroquois with their five nations — later six — were concentrated for the most part in central New York State. Yet they claimed dominance by right of conquest over nearly all the tribes from Hudson Bay to the Tennessee River, and westward to Lake Michigan and the Illinois River. Probably no other Indian government north of Mexico was so complete and so splendidly adapted to permit the fullest measure of freedom to each component tribe, while securing united action in all that pertained to the whole. The Iroquois government has been compared to our own system of independent state and federal governments. The Iroquois were divided into eight families, irrespective of nationality, each having its distinct emblem or totem. Thus, intimately mingled in one village might be Mohawks, Oneidas, Onondagas, Cayugas, and Senecas, all members being of the Turtle clan and all being aflame with Iroquois patriotism. This stratum of connection by clan or family was very strong and served as an eightfold chain binding the five nations into a closely knit league.

The principal chiefs, or sachems, varied in number from eight to fourteen in the several nations. The sachems of the five nations, fifty in all, when assembled in council formed the government of the confederacy. There was also a class of subordinate chiefs, not hereditary, as were the sachems, but rising to office by ability or valor. This class, consisting of each nation's best talent, held its own councils and exercised an influence proportionate to its numbers and abilities.

There was still another council, essentially popular in the sense that any man who qualified by age, wisdom, and experience could participate in it. It represented on a democratic scale the gathered wisdom of the nation. The Jesuit Lafitau compares it to the Roman Senate in the early, rude age of the Republic and asserts that it loses nothing in the comparison. "It is a greasy assemblage," he reports, "sitting *sur leur derrière*, crouched like apes, their knees as high as their ears, or lying, some on their bellies, some on their backs, each with a pipe in his mouth, discussing affairs of state with as much coolness and gravity as the Spanish Junta or the Grand Council of Venice."

The young warriors also had their councils; so, too, had the women. The opinions of both these groups were presented by deputies to the higher councils and were given due consideration. No alien could become a member of the tribe except by formal adoption into the clan, and as the right of adoption rested solely with the women as mothers of the clan, it was upon their will that hung the fate of captives, whether for life or death.

The Iroquois settled all questions by councils — social, political, military, religious. As a consequence of numerous councils with them that tapped the experience, thought, and wisdom of virtually all individuals, the civilized contemporaries of the Iroquois were compelled to marvel at their practiced astuteness. "It is by a most subtle policy," says Lafitau, "that they have taken the ascendant over the other nations, divided and overcome the most warlike, made themselves a terror to the most remote, and now hold a peaceful neutrality between the French and English, courted and feared by both."

Probably not since the days of ancient Sparta had individual life and national life been more completely fused into one, and flaming nationalism more solidly engendered. After a careful study of their complex system of government, Parkman concludes that the Iroquois method of legislation "organized the chaotic past and gave concrete forms to Indian nature itself. The people have dwindled and decayed; but, banded by its ties of clan and kin, the league in feeble miniature still subsists, and the degenerate Iroquois looks back with a mournful pride to the glory of the past."

If an individual was guilty of treason or by his conduct rendered himself dangerous or obnoxious to the public, the council of chiefs met in secret session on his case, condemned him to death, and designated some brave to execute him. Watching his opportunity, the executioner brained him or stabbed him unawares, usually in the dark porch of one of the houses. Since he acted by public authority, the relatives of the slain man had no redress, even if they desired it.

According to Iroquois tradition, as interpreted by J.N.B. Hewitt, the league or confederacy was established through the efforts of Hiawatha (River Maker), probably of the Mohawk tribe, about 1570, or approximately forty years before the appearance of the French and Dutch in their country. At this time, they numbered altogether probably fewer than six thousand, with formidable and aggressive enemies all around them, notably the Algonquins.

In 1609 Champlain made the mistake, innocent but fatal, of allying himself with the Algonquins when they invaded the Iroquois country. The help thus extended by the French, enabling the Algonquin to win the victory, was never forgotten nor forgiven by the vengeful Iroquois. Indeed, from that day they become the constant, unrelenting enemies of the French, and to this fact was largely due the defeat of French ambitions in Canada.

In that initial battle with the French, the Iroquois learned the lesson of the deadly effectiveness of firearms. Through the Dutch at Albany in 1615, they supplied themselves with guns and quickly inaugurated a systematic war of conquest or extermination against all the surrounding tribes, particularly those in league with the French. Henceforth the menace of the Iroquois was to hang like a pall over the wilderness of New France, and their war cry would send terror into the souls of the French and their Indian allies for many years to come.

Champlain spent a winter with the Hurons and saw their squalor and superstition. The spectacle aroused his sympathy and prompted him to take measures to end their spiritual desolation. Accordingly he appealed to the Franciscan Récollets to bring to them the truths and blessings of the Christian Faith. In response, the Récollets crossed the Atlantic and began their labors among the aborigines of Georgian Bay.

In the early summer of 1615, the Récollet Joseph Le Caron journeyed up the Ottawa, over Lake Nipissing, and down the French River to the Huron country. He pitched a rough shelter at Carhagouha, a few miles west of Penetanguishene, and there on August 15 said Mass, the first ever celebrated in the present Province of Ontario. Other members of his order, including Brother Gabriel Sagard, who published the first history of early Canada, came to work among the Hurons.

Two of the Récollets remained at Quebec to minister to the colonists and the neighboring Indians. For ten years they journeyed fearlessly among the various tribes; they opened a school for young Indians and summoned recruits from France. Among the latter was Father Nicholas Viel, who was hurled into the Ottawa River by an apostate Indian and drowned in the rapids at the spot that still bears the name Sault-au-Récollet.

Realizing that the Huron field was too vast for them to till alone, the Récollets sent a delegate to France to invite the Society of Jesus to come to their aid. In response, the Jesuits sent Fathers Jean de Brébeuf, Charles Lalemant, and Enemond Massé, who arrived in New France in 1625. The following year, Brébeuf, with another recently landed Jesuit, Father Anne de Noüe, and the Récollet Father Joseph de Daillon, paddled up the Ottawa River to Huronia to continue the work begun by the sons of St. Francis.

After a year of hardship and privation, de Noüe and Daillon returned to Quebec, leaving Brébeuf alone in the Huron wilderness. He, too, was recalled, in 1629, when the British seized the French colony at Quebec and shipped all the missionaries back to France.

The treaty of St. Germain-en-Laye having restored Canada to France in 1632, the Jesuit fathers returned "to work for the

Hurons," as one of their chroniclers phrased it, "suffer every evil, and complain only to God."

Father Paul Le Jeune organized religious services at Quebec, founded a mission at Three Rivers, and in 1635 opened the College of Quebec. Other Jesuits had in the meantime established a mission at Miscou, an island at the entrance of the Baie des Chaleurs, whence they evangelized Gaspé, Acadia, and Cape Breton. When on Christmas Day in 1635 Champlain lay dying in the arms of his friend Father Charles Lalemant, he rejoiced that the Christian Faith had already gained a foothold in the territory he had opened.

Such is the historical background. In the century and a half since Cabot had visited the shores of Canada, few immigrants had come from France, and the services of religion were conducted in but a few lonely outposts among the Indians. A great continent stretched out before the missionaries, challenging them to penetrate its virgin forests and bring the good tidings of the gospel to its dwellers. The booming of the cannon at the little fort at Quebec now sounded not only a welcome to incoming passengers on the French sailing ships but also the ending of the long prologue to the American drama.

The curtain had fallen on the long night, a night stretching through uncounted centuries, in which not a line of history had been written on rock or on parchment; the curtain was rising on the new scene, with Christianity and European civilization advancing upon the wilderness. Onto the stage of New France stepped the missionaries whose heroic zeal was to win for them the imperishable crown of martyrdom.

Book Two

~

Isaac Jogues
René Goupil
Jean de Lalande

~

Chapter 2

Of the Jesuit priests who surrendered their lives in North America, Isaac Jogues was the first. He was also the first priest to enter what is now New York State and the first to visit New Amsterdam, where he dwelt for a time with the Dutch. He and Charles Raymbault penetrated as far as Sault Sainte Marie and were, as Bancroft points out, "the first missionaries to preach the gospel a thousand miles in the interior, five years before John Eliot addressed the Indians six miles from Boston Harbor."

Jogues was of medium height, slender, and wiry. He was born in Orléans, France, on January 10, 1607, of well-to-do parents, Laurent and Françoise Jogues. When he had completed his college course at seventeen, he entered the novitiate of the Society of Jesus at Rouen. Asked what he sought in entering the Society, he replied, "Ethiopia and martyrdom."

"Not so, my child," replied Father Louis Lallemant. "You will die in Canada."

For three years, Jogues studied philosophy at La Flèche, where Father Enemond Massé had aroused great interest in the missions. Massé had gone to the mission in Acadia in 1611, only to be shipped back two years later by the English. Jogues taught at the College of Rouen for four years, after which he entered Clermont College in Paris to study theology. He was ordained in 1636, early enough in the year to be ready to sail that spring for New France. He celebrated his first Mass on February 10 at Orléans, in the presence of his family.

His widowed mother watched through tear-dimmed eyes as he ascended the altar to pronounce for the first time the words of consecration. The words *mon cher Isaac*, which she had often murmured over him when he was a child, were on her lips again. At Communion time, she knelt at the rail, and her son placed the Host upon her tongue.

Perhaps from intuition of his final end, perhaps from anguish at being parted from him, Jogues's mother pleaded with him for days to remain in France, at least for a time. "I am growing old," she said, "and I want you near me for a few years. I have loved you most of all my children. I have seen so little of you the past twelve years. You break my heart going away to spend your life with those wild barbarians in the wilderness so far away."

Placing his arms tenderly around her shoulders, he said, "Mother, you know how dearly I love you — and will always love you. . . . But God is calling me to do His work, to bring His truths to the pagan tribes of America, who do not know Him. We are both making the sacrifice — and a big one. But God will not be outdone in generosity. He will not fail to reward those who give their all, even their lives, for Him."

Just before sailing from Dieppe, he wrote a letter to his "honored mother," begging her to submit her will generously to the divine will. "For a little gain," he writes, "some men traverse the seas, enduring at least as much as we; and shall we not for the love of God do what these men do for earthly interests? Goodbye, dear

Mother. I thank you for all the great love that you have always given me, and especially for the love you showed at our last meeting. May God reunite us in His holy Paradise if we do not ever see each other here on earth."

≈

On the morning of July 2, 1636, Father Isaac Jogues stood on the deck of a French sailing vessel as it edged into Quebec harbor. The beetling cliff rose high out of the gray mists, like the wall of a fortress; from its top waved the French tricolor. The booming cannon welcomed the voyagers to the chief settlement of New France, and at the wharf a cluster of people waved and shouted greetings.

Jogues felt his heart pound with excitement as he spied on the shore a number of bronze-colored Indians. Never had he laid eyes on such strange-looking creatures, with their faces and half-naked bodies grotesquely streaked with bright colors; with their heavy features — large, hooked noses, bulbous lips, high cheekbones — their dark eyes that peered through narrow slits, their black, straight, coarse hair that reminded him of a horse's mane. So these, he thought, were to be his clients. These were the people he had come to evangelize, to serve, perhaps to die for.

His amazement gave way to rapture and joy. "I do not know what it is to enter Paradise," he wrote a few hours later to his mother, "but this I know, that it would be difficult to experience in this world a joy more excessive and more overflowing than that I felt when I set my foot in New France and celebrated my first Mass here at Quebec on the feast of the Visitation. I assure you, it was indeed a day of the visitation of the goodness of God and our Lady. I felt as if it were a Christmas Day for me, and that I was to be born again to a new life, and a life in God."

After he had landed, Jogues and a brother Jesuit, Du Marche, climbed the dirt road along the bank of the St. Charles to the residence of the Jesuit fathers, Notre Dame des Anges. This was a mile or two away, near the little river Lairet. Here he became a member of a household that comprised Brébeuf, Massé, Antoine Daniel, Ambroise Davost, De Nouë, and Le Jeune — names destined to be written in large and shining letters in the history of New France.

In this crude structure which was Notre Dame des Anges, the Fathers laid the plan of winning to Christianity a kingdom that would stretch from the Atlantic to the nameless western sea, from the Arctic to the Gulf of Mexico. "Here," observes Parkman, "was nourished the germ of a vast enterprise, and this was the cradle of the mission of New France. . . . These men aimed at the conversion of a continent. From their hovel on the St. Charles, they surveyed a field of labor whose vastness might tire the wings of thought itself; a scene repellent and appalling, darkened with omens of peril and woe. They were an advance-guard of the great army of Loyola, strong in a discipline that controlled not alone the body and the will, but the intellect, the heart, the soul, and the inmost consciousness. The lives of these early Canadian Jesuits attest the earnestness of their faith and the intensity of their zeal; but it was a zeal bridled, curbed, and ruled by a guiding hand. Their marvelous training in equal measure kindled enthusiasm and controlled it. . . . One great aim engrossed their lives: For the greater glory of God — *ad majorem Dei gloriam.*"[4]

In outlining their plan for evangelizing the Indian tribes, the Jesuit fathers decided to concentrate first upon the Hurons, and it was to them that Jogues requested to be sent. Ten days later, Jogues,

[4] Parkman, *The Jesuits in North America,* 5 ff.

with a party of Jesuit priests and an eleven-year-old boy, Jean Amyot, was paddling up the St. Lawrence to Three Rivers. This was an ancient trading place of the Indians, and here Jogues was to await a flotilla of Hurons, in the hope of returning with them to their own region. The Hurons had been trading with the French for many years at Three Rivers, and always under difficulties; the Algonquins controlled the passage to Three Rivers, and they exacted tribute from the Hurons bringing their wares to the French.

While waiting there, Jogues had a glimpse of Indian savagery that made him shudder. A flotilla of Algonquins came down the river, singing and banging their paddles against the sides of their birchbark canoes. Twenty-eight scalp-locks fluttered from upright poles, and in one boat a captive Iroquois Indian stood shouting defiance. As soon as he stepped ashore, the Algonquins — men, women, and children — leaped upon him. They beat him with clubs, cut him with knives, bit off his fingers, thrust flaming torches against his flesh, and rammed one down his throat.

Father Le Jeune, the superior of the little French party, rushed toward them and commanded them to stop, threatening to withdraw his friendship from the Algonquin Indians. The torture was brought to an end, but the Indians led the captive Iroquois away for final treatment. An age-old custom was not to be eradicated in a moment.

About a week later, the Hurons were allowed passage down to Three Rivers. In the first canoe was the bearded figure of the Jesuit Father Antoine Daniel, a pathetic sight. He was gaunt and haggard, his eyes were sunken, his cassock in shreds, his breviary hanging from a string around his neck. He seemed a living skeleton. But he sprang ashore, smiling and lighthearted, and embraced his friends and welcomed Jogues, the recruit who had come to bolster the thin battle line.

Saints of the American Wilderness

Father Daniel was to continue on to Quebec, and it was arranged that Jogues should take the veteran's place on the Hurons'
return journey three days hence. On Sunday, August 24, he said
Mass, bade farewell to the Fathers, and with singing heart stepped
into the fragile birchbark to begin the long trek to Huronia. With
him went Jean Amyot.

The journey was full of hardships. They had to carry boats, provisions, and luggage around fifty cascades. For distances of four,
eight, and ten miles they dragged the canoes through rapids where
the water came to their waists and sometimes even to their necks.
They lived on one meal a day, consisting of a little ground Indian
corn mixed with water. They slept on rocks and in the woods.
Jogues had to carry Jean Amyot on his shoulders part of the way,
for the boy had become sick. The party was plagued by mosquitoes, and they had to be on constant guard against lurking Iroquois. At last, aching in every limb but with courage undaunted,
Father Jogues and his party staggered through the triple stockade
of the Indian town of Ihonatiria. Here the priest fell into the arms
of Father Brébeuf and his companions, whose joy knew no bounds.
It was September 11; he had made the nine-hundred-mile trek in
nineteen days.

Ihonatiria was a picture of filth and decay. The Indians' cabins
were littered with dirt, fish, bones, furs, scalps, refuse, and dogs. At
mealtimes and at night they were crowded with men and women
who were strangers to elementary sanitation. The stench was un-
bearable. The dirt floor upon which everyone reclined was crawling with vermin. Smoke from the invariable fires inflamed the
eyes, and if visiting missionaries reclined on the floor, dogs and
children crawled over them, completing the litany of discomfort.

There now were eleven Frenchmen in the village: six priests,
four workmen, and Jean Amyot. They gathered together into a

cabin, called St. Joseph's, where the new arrivals, Jogues and Jean, were stared at by the throngs of curious Indians of all ages who swarmed through the cabin.

When the last of them had left, Father Jean de Brébeuf, who was the superior and the veteran missionary among the Hurons, addressed Jogues and two other recent arrivals, Fathers Garnier and Chastellain, concerning the mission: "Instead of being a great master and a great theologian, as in France," he said, "you must reckon on being here a humble scholar; and then, good God, with what masters! — women, little children, and all the savages — and exposed to what laughter! The Huron language will be your Saint Thomas and your Aristotle. Clever men as you are, and speaking glibly among learned and capable persons, you must make up your minds to be mute for a long time among the barbarians. You will have accomplished much if you begin to stammer a little at the end of a considerable time."

Brébeuf prepared them for the continual discomforts in store for them: piercing cold, smoke that would so inflame their eyes that they could read no more than a few lines of their breviary at a time, coarse and unpalatable food, the ever-present danger of death. He warned them of the mischievous sorcerers, jealous, resentful and treacherous, who might at any moment incite the natives against them.

"You must realize," he said, "that our lives depend upon a single thread. We are told to expect death every hour and be prepared for it, no matter where we are in the world; that applies here particularly. . . . The malice of the savages gives us special cause for almost perpetual fear; a malcontent may burn you down or may cleave your head open in some lonely spot. Then, too, we are responsible for the sterility or the fecundity of the earth, under the penalty of our lives. We are the cause of droughts; if we cannot make rain, they speak of nothing less than murdering us. It is to souls like yours that God has appointed the conquest of many other souls. . . . Fear no difficulties; there will be none for you, since it is your whole consolation to see yourself crucified with the Son of God."

~

Within a week of his arrival, Jogues was stricken with an ill-ness, apparently a form of influenza. Without medicine or reme-dies of any kind, he soon had a burning fever and ached all over. He bled profusely from the nostrils, and his condition became critical.

For several days he hovered between life and death. Soon the other missionaries were stricken; it was an epidemic, and it swept through the whole northern section of the Huron peninsula, tak-ing hundreds of lives.

Ihonatiria was swept with a tidal wave of fear, hysteria, and mad-ness. The Indians appealed to their medicine men to drive the sickness away. When their incantations, dancing, and shouting proved futile, the sorcerers put the blame for the pestilence and for their own failure on the missionaries and urged that they be put to death.

The epidemic was especially severe at the larger village of Ossossané, about twelve miles away. The Huron chiefs were as-sembled there, deliberating upon when and how the priests were to be killed. Brébeuf boldly walked to Ossossané and into their midst. He pleaded, remonstrated, and explained, but was listened to in gloomy silence.

The threats of vengeance grew louder. The missionaries, fear-ing that their death was a matter of hours, withdrew to Father Paul Ragueneau's hut and wrote a letter of farewell to their superior at

Quebec. Their only regret, they wrote, was that they had not been able to suffer more for the Faith. The letter was entrusted to a faithful Indian, who brought it to its destination.

For reasons not known, the Indians did not carry out their threats. But every moment was filled with terror: "The missionaries," observes Parkman, "were like men who trod on the lava-crust of a volcano palpitating with the throes of a coming eruption, while the molten death beneath their feet gleamed white-hot from a thousand crevices."

All winter the priests ministered to the natives. They visited the sick and cared for them in the best way they could. Through it all, however, they knew from the sullen looks of many of the braves that the tomahawk might fall upon them at any moment of the day or night. By spring the epidemic had passed, and conditions improved. At the year's end, Jogues had written to his mother, "We have baptized about 240 of them this year. . . . All the labors of a million persons, would they not be worthwhile if they gained one single soul for Jesus Christ?"

With the end of the plague, the Indians abandoned Ihonatiria. Upon the little river Wye, which flows into Georgian Bay — the eastern arm of Lake Huron — the Fathers, under their new superior, Jerome Lalemant, brother of Charles, established the mission of Sainte Marie. It was fortified and included a storehouse for provisions, a place of refuge for fugitive Indians, and a home from which the missionaries could fan out to the chief settlements in Huronia. It was to be for many years the center of their far-flung missionary work, the place for which they would always manifest the strongest attachment.

The priests cultivated the land adjacent to the fortified settlement and taught the Indians the arts of agriculture and husbandry. They kept fowl, swine, and cattle, and how they managed to transport the beasts through nearly a thousand miles of wilderness is a marvel. The settlement was a blessing for the natives; at times, three and even four thousand were fed and sheltered within the walls. They were instructed in Christianity, and they assisted at services in the mission church.

The Fathers converged upon this central mission from their stations scattered throughout Huronia. They came for retreats and for conferences in which they would plan how to carry the gospel ever deeper into the interior. Francis Parkman has graphically described the mission, and so vivid is his account of the Jesuit Fathers in their new mission home that it is well worth quoting at length, making allowances for his want of spiritual appreciation:

Hither, while the Fathers are gathered from their scattered stations at one of their periodical meetings, let us, too, repair and join them. We enter at the eastern gate of the fortification, midway in the wall between its northern and southern bastions, and pass to the hall, where at a rude table, spread with ruder fare, all the household are assembled — laborers, domestics, soldiers, priests. It was a scene that might recall a remote half-feudal, half-patriarchal age, when under the smoky rafters of his antique hall some warlike thane sat, with kinsmen and dependents, ranged down the long board, each in his degree. Here doubtless Ragueneau, the Father Superior, held the place of honor; and for chieftains, scarred with Danish battleaxes, was seen a band of thoughtful men clad in threadbare garb of black, their brows swarthy from exposure, yet marked with the lines of intellect and a fixed enthusiasm of purpose. Here was Bressani, scarred with firebrand and knife; Chabanel, once a professor of rhetoric in France, now a missionary bound by a

self-imposed vow to a life from which his nature recoiled. . . .
Garnier, beardless like a woman, was of a far finer nature.
His religion was of the affections and the sentiments; and
his imagination, warmed with the ardor of his faith, shaped
the ideal form of his worship into visible realities.

Brébeuf sat conspicuous among his brethren, portly and
tall, his short moustache and beard grizzled — for he was
fifty-six years old. If he seemed impassive, it was because
one overmastering principle had merged and absorbed all
the impulses of his nature and all the faculties of his mind.
The enthusiasm which with many are fitful was with him
the current of his life — solemn and deep as the tide of des-
tiny. The Divine Trinity, the Virgin, the Saints, Heaven
and Hell, Angels and Fiends — to him these alone were
real; all else were naught.

Gabriel Lalemant, nephew of Jerome Lalemant, Superior at Quebec, was Brébeuf's colleague at the mission of St.
Ignace. His slender frame and delicate features gave him an
appearance of youth, though he had reached middle life;
and, as in the case of Garnier, the fervor of his mind sustained him through exertions of which he seemed physically incapable.

Of the rest of that company little has come down to us
but the bare record of their missionary toils; and we may ask
in vain what youthful enthusiasm, what broken hope or
faded dream, turned the current of their lives, and sent them
from the heart of civilization to the savage outpost of the
world. No element was wanting in them for the achievement of such a success as that to which they aspired — neither the transcendental zeal, nor a matchless discipline, nor
a practical sagacity very seldom surpassed in the pursuits

where men strive for wealth and place, and if they were destined to disappointment, it was the result of external causes, against which no power of theirs could have insured them.[5]

It was no broken hope or faded dream that had sent them; it was a living faith in Christ and a readiness to carry out His command: "Going, therefore, teach ye all nations."[6]

One could wish that Parkman had included Jogues among the characters described: it was Isaac's practical sagacity that had prompted his superiors to put him in charge of construction at Sainte Marie.

From headquarters at Sainte Marie, Jogues and Garnier went forth to evangelize the Petun, or Tobacco, tribe. On the way, they were abandoned by their guides. It was the dead of winter, and they were obliged to make their beds in the snow. They reached the first encampment of the Petuns and were promptly driven away by the excited Indians, who apparently had been warned that the Blackrobes were evil sorcerers. They went from village to village, followed by the natives, who hurled threats and imprecations. In the end, they were able to baptize only one old squaw, and they returned to Sainte Marie. Whether it was through the prayers or example of the baptized squaw, a change of heart came over the Petuns, and the following year Garnier returned and was able to found a successful mission among them.

In 1641 a throng of Ojibways, or Chippewas, came from Lake Superior to participate in the great decennial feast of the dead with the Hurons. Astonished by the mission and its success among the Hurons, they requested that a mission be established in their

---

[5] Parkman, *The Jesuits in North America*, 369 ff.
[6] Matt. 28:19.

own country. Accordingly, Jogues and Raymbault were assigned to them. They began the long trek on September 17, paddling for weeks along the eastern shore of Georgian Bay and the upper reaches of Lake Huron. After many perils and almost constant hardship, they arrived at a place they called Sault Sainte Marie, now the center of commerce which bears that name. Jogues and Raymbault were the first white men to stand on the shores of Lake Superior. Jean Nicolet, the explorer, had preceded them into this general region, but he had gone down through the Straits of Mackinac and explored Lake Michigan, while they kept to the north and west.

The priests were well received by the Chippewas. Jogues addressed in their own language an assembly of two thousand, explaining to them the principal teachings of the Christian religion. He assured them that after he had reported back to his superior, he and another priest would plant a mission there. "Then, after instructing you," he added, pointing toward the west, "we shall go thither." He erected a great cross facing the country of the Sioux, who were settled about the headwaters of the Mississippi.

Indeed, as Jogues and Raymbault gazed westward over the wide waters of Lake Superior, their hearts burned with a desire to penetrate to the lands beyond, where they might proclaim the gospel to the tribes dwelling there — the Sioux, the Crees, and the Illinois — who had never seen a white man.

Their Huron guides were getting restless. They wanted to start on the return journey to Sainte Marie before the October storms should add to the difficulties of their journey. Reluctantly, the two Blackrobes bade goodbye to their Chippewa friends and started out for home. Three weeks later, after incredible perils and hardships, suffering from hunger and from the elements, they reached their brethren.

Jogues and Raymbault urged that missionaries be sent far to the west to evangelize those nations which they were convinced, on the basis of their Chippewa experiences, would be hospitable and receptive to the gospel. "But we need more laborers for that purpose," replied Father Jerome Lalemant, the superior. "We must first try to win the peoples who are nearest to us and meanwhile pray Heaven to hasten the moment of their conversion." Their first endeavor, he explained, must be to succeed with the Hurons. Only then, in God's good time, should they extend the mission to the western nations.

At Sainte Marie, resuming his ministry, Father Jogues was gratified to observe the increasing friendliness and reverence on the part of the Hurons. Apart from the understanding treatment they received at Sainte Marie, the Hurons had other reasons to be impressed with the Jesuit Fathers. Their braves had reported, for example, how the French in Quebec, including their governor, Montmagny, listened to the Blackrobes and heeded their advice. Moreover, at the council held that summer at Three Rivers, Montmagny had explained to the Hurons present that the gifts he offered them were to serve as reminders of the truth of the gospel preached by the missionaries. The Hurons, deeply impressed, flocked in greater numbers and with growing respect to Sainte Marie.

Adults were admitted to Baptism only after lengthy instruction and unmistakable proof of sincerity. It needed heroic virtue for an Indian to live a Christian life amid the immorality and degradation of his surroundings. Even so, many of the converts astonished the missionaries with their staunch devotion. "I must say," wrote one of the Fathers at the neighboring mission of Ossossané, that here is seen, through the grace of God, a Church established, and Christians who not only live in the practice of the Faith, but who in the midst of Satan's reign, triumph over impiety itself."

It was the practice of the missionaries to bring the Indians to the central mission of Sainte Marie for Baptism. There, on the great feast days of the Church, neophytes were baptized with solemn ceremonies before great throngs. Thither came one of the greatest war chiefs of all the Hurons, Ahatsistari, who had begged to be admitted into the Church. His feats had made him a hero and the most highly honored of Huron warriors. On Holy Saturday 1642, he and a number of other Hurons were received by Jogues and the other missionaries into the Church. Ahatsistari was baptized Eustace.

It was a day of rejoicing for Blackrobes and Redskins alike. At last Christianity was beginning to take root in the American forest. The day would soon dawn, perhaps, when the bloodcurdling war whoop of the Indian brave, the upraised tomahawk, the crackle of fagots, and the shrieks of the victim would no longer be known.

"As to the state of Christianity in these countries," wrote Jerome Lalemant in his official report of that year, "I may truly say that the Church is gaining strength in numbers and still more in sanctity; that the Holy Spirit is working as visibly here as in any place in this New World; and that one would admire such faith, such piety, such courage as we witness here among some of the barbarians, even though it was manifested in persons brought up from the cradle amid examples of virtue and religion."

Father Jogues was happy garnering the harvest at Sainte Marie. But he wanted to do and to suffer more to increase the harvest. Long accustomed to spending much time before the Blessed Sacrament, he now redoubled the fervor of his prayers. He begged for the conversion of all the Hurons and asked for an occasion to prove his love of God and of souls. He pondered often the saying of the early Christians: "The blood of martyrs is the seed of Christians." Gladly would he give his own blood.

Kneeling alone before the altar, Jogues felt an overwhelming desire to suffer for God, to undergo hardship, to offer himself — body, mind, and soul — as a clean oblation for the sins of men, as a means of planting the Faith deep in the hearts of the Indians. Emotion stirred him to the depths. When finally it subsided, he heard a voice within him saying over and over, "Thy prayer is heard. Be it done to thee as thou hast asked. Be comforted; be of strong heart."

Jogues had no doubt that God had spoken to him. "These words," he wrote, "had issued from the lips of Him with whom saying and doing are only one and the same thing." Jogues had offered himself, and God had accepted the offering. He knew that the words that came in reply were revelation and prophecy.

~

Chapter 3

In June certain of the Huron leaders were preparing for their trading expedition to the French settlements. As Sainte Marie was badly in need of supplies, it was necessary to send a priest along with them. The Iroquois were on the warpath and had been reported at various points along the St. Lawrence. Father Lalemant knew, therefore, that he was virtually condemning to death whomever he should select for the journey. He chose Isaac Jogues, but left him free to accept or reject the mission.

Jogues accepted without hesitation, understanding perfectly the dangers he faced. Indeed, he felt that God had in this way accepted his offer and was preparing him for some extraordinary trial. "Gladly and willingly," he wrote, "did I accept the charge laid before me by obedience and charity. I offered myself with all my heart; and that the more willingly, because the necessity of undertaking this journey might have cast some other of the Fathers, much more valuable than I, into the perils and hazards of which we were all aware."

The greatest of these perils, of course, arose from the large numbers of Iroquois lurking along the waterways. Dread of these marauders hung like a pall over river and forest, doubly so because their deadly effectiveness was heightened by the muskets the Dutch were selling to them. Back in Quebec, Father Vimont, the superior there, declared that the traders who put firearms in the hands of such vengeful Indians "deserve the punishment due to all the crimes which the avarice of the one party and the fury of the other have engendered."

The Iroquois were willing to sign a treaty of peace with the French, but they expressed implacable hatred of the Hurons and Algonquins and would be content with nothing short of their complete extermination. The French refused to abandon their allies, but neither did they consider it advisable to entrust firearms into the hands of the Indians. Hence, the Iroquois began to loose their fury indiscriminately upon the Indians and the French.

That Jogues was aware of the Iroquois attitude is evident from a letter in which he wrote that "these Iroquois swore if they ever took another Frenchman captive, they would burn him alive over a slow fire, in the same way that they inflict the direst tortures on their other prisoners."

Early in the morning of June 13, 1642, Jogues and Raymbault said their Masses and gave Holy Communion to the French and Hurons who were to accompany them. The party comprised twenty Hurons under the war chief Eustace Ahatsistari, and five Frenchmen: the two priests, two workmen, and William Couture, who as a layman had dedicated his life to the service of the missions. They traveled in four canoes, and after thirty-five days, in continuous fear of the Iroquois, they reached Three Rivers. From there they pushed on safely to Quebec.

There Jogues pleaded for more laborers. But no missionaries had come from France since 1641, and Father Vimont was unable to send more. He could not even replace Raymbault, who was dying from tuberculosis contracted during his long journeys, and breathed his last a few months later. Raymbault was buried by the side of Champlain, but the site of their graves is not known.

Father Vimont agreed to spare a young *donné*, René Goupil, who had accompanied William Couture from France in 1640. Goupil was thirty-four and had been ministering to the sick among the French and Indians at Quebec. As a young man, he had spent several months in the Jesuit novitiate in Paris, intending to study for the priesthood. Illness had forced him to leave, much to his own regret and that of the Jesuits. He studied medicine and surgery and, after a successful practice of some years, had offered himself as a *donné* for the Huron mission.

A *donné* bound himself by contract and by a private, not religious, vow for life "to serve and assist the Fathers who work for the salvation and conversion of souls" in the Indian missions. He promised to live in obedience, poverty, and chastity; in return, he was guaranteed food, clothing, and shelter, in substantially the same manner as were the missionaries. The *donnés* were valuable helpers, fitting in between the lay brothers, who were bound by religious vows, and the *engagés,* or hired workmen, bound by no vow at all.

Through his tireless ministry to the sick, René Goupil had won the esteem and affection of both the French and the Indians. When he was invited to embark with Jogues, being reminded of the dangers in store for him, he accepted instantly and with the same humble generosity that had endeared him to all at Quebec. He had left France, he said, to labor among the Hurons and was ready to share the hardships that fell to the lot of the missionaries. Jogues was delighted; in Goupil and Couture he had devoted assistants for the trying days ahead.

At last Jogues secured the supplies needed for Sainte Marie and the thirty-five people who would be living there for the coming year. With him on the return trip was also, besides other members of the party, an Indian girl of thirteen, Theresa. She was the niece of Joseph Teondechoren, one of the Huron chiefs accompanying Jogues. Theresa had been educated by the Ursuline nuns at Quebec and was returning to her people to assist in spreading the Faith.

In view of the danger from the Iroquois, the governor offered a detachment of soldiers to convoy the flotilla. The Hurons, however, contended that they were able to take care of themselves.

They reached Three Rivers safely and pushed on again on August 1, 1642. After a day's journey, they noticed footprints on the shore. "If it is the trail of friends," said Eustace Ahatsistari, "we have no fear; if it is an enemy's, we are strong enough to conquer." They had continued but a short distance when suddenly they heard war whoops and a volley of musketry. A war party of about thirty Mohawks, members of the Iroquois federation, led by a former Huron who had been captured by the Iroquois and was now one of them, swooped down upon the canoes out of ambush. The pilot of Jogues's canoe, Atieronhonk, was hit in the hand by a bullet. The priest, heedless of his own safety, scrambled to his assistance. Atieronhonk had previously received instruction, but not Baptism, and this he now requested. Cupping water in his hand, Jogues poured it over his head, baptizing him Bernard. The Indian later escaped and never ceased praising the missionary.

"Ondessonk [Bird of Prey] forgot himself at the sight of danger," he would exclaim. "He thought only of me and of my salvation; he feared not to lose his own life, but feared lest I should be lost forever."

The Hurons in the rear canoes turned quickly and fled. Those in the front canoes, caught in the fusillade, reached the shore and fought desperately with spears and arrows against a foe armed with muskets. To their consternation, another band of forty Mohawks closed in on them from the rear.

Jogues had been dumped from his canoe into the tall weeds. Under their concealment he could have crawled into the woods and escaped. But he spurned the thought, knowing his place was at the side of his stricken flock. He had just seen Goupil fighting furiously against tremendous odds, only to be overwhelmed at last. Jogues, to the amazement of the Iroquois, arose from the weeds and strode into their midst.

Couture had escaped into the woods, but suddenly realized that Jogues was not with him. He deliberately returned to be with his spiritual leader. Five Iroquois closed in on him. One of them snapped his gun at Couture's breast, but it missed fire. In the excitement, Couture fired his own gun and the Indian fell dead. The others now assaulted him with unrestrained vengeance. They stripped him, tore out all his fingernails, gnawed his fingers, and drove a sword through his right hand.

Rushing to his side, Jogues took the wounded man in his arms. "Offer up all your pain to Almighty God, dear William," he said. "He will give you the strength to bear it, and He will reward you a thousandfold." Writhing in agony, Couture made no sound of complaint.

The Iroquois at first looked on the unusual proceedings in wonder; then, regaining their senses, they leaped upon the priest and beat him with fists, clubs, and sticks until he fell unconscious. When he came to, they bit out his fingernails and chewed his two forefingers. René Goupil they treated similarly.

The Iroquois started binding the prisoners: three Frenchmen and twenty Hurons. Three Hurons bad been killed. Jogues assured the Iroquois there was no need to tie him. "As long as these friends of mine are in your hands," he said, "nothing could make me flee."

They left him unbound, and while they continued their work on the others and were dividing the plunder in the captured canoes, Jogues circulated among the prisoners and ministered to them. A few of the Hurons had not been baptized, and some now wished to receive the sacrament. Jogues completed their instruction, with his mangled fingers squeezed water from his wet clothing, and baptized them. "Put your trust in God," he admonished them. "He will give you the courage and strength to endure this ordeal."

Jogues knelt at the side of Goupil, who was bleeding profusely. "Dearest brother," he said, "God has acted strangely toward us. But He is the Lord and the Master. What is good in His eyes, that He has done. As it has pleased Him, so be it. Blessed is His Holy Name forever."

Among the captives was Eustace Ahatsistari. Upon him and upon the other Huron leaders, now captive, the Fathers had pinned much of their hope for the speedy conversion of the Hurons and their Indian allies. It would be a tragic setback for the mission at Sainte Marie.

The Iroquois were leaving the Huron prisoners untouched for the time being. They seemed concerned for the present with taking their revenge upon the French, whose people had refused to accept their peace terms.

When the Iroquois ordered the captives into the canoes, one old warrior refused. "What!" he exclaimed. "Shall I, a hoary old man, go to a strange and foreign land? Never! Here I will die." They slew him on the spot where he had been baptized a few minutes before.

With joyful shouts, the Iroquois embarked with their captives and crossed, under a burning sun, to the mouth of the river Richelieu, where the town of Sorel now stands, and there they encamped. Later they pushed up the Richelieu to Lake Champlain, then by way of Lake George to the Mohawk settlements. The priest and his two French companions were the first white men to gaze upon Lake George.

The wounds of Jogues and his two Frenchmen were putrefying by then, and their condition was intensified by the swarming mosquitoes, which gave them no rest by day or by night. Five or six days later, some of the braves approached them in their exhausted condition and proceeded to pluck out their hair and beards and to drive their long fingernails into the most sensitive parts of their bodies.

"Much more was I shaken by the interior anguish," laments Jogues, "when I saw this funereal procession of our Christians led before my very eyes, this cortège of death in which were the five tried Christians, the sustaining columns of the Church among the Hurons. Indeed, and I confess it honestly, time and time again I could not restrain my tears, grieving over the lot of these poor Hurons and of my French comrades, and worrying terribly about the things that might happen in the future. I had before my eyes continually the sight of the door of the Christian Faith among the Hurons and other innumerable nations closed by these Iroquois, unless it might be opened by a most extraordinary dispensation of Divine Providence. This thought made me die every hour, in the depth of my soul. It is a hard thing — more, it is a cruel thing — to bear, that of seeing the triumph of the demons over whole nations redeemed with so much love, and paid for in the money of a Blood so adorable."

On the third or fourth day, as Jogues, Couture, and Goupil sat huddled in the canoe, René disclosed his desire to pronounce the vows that would admit him as a lay member of the Society of Jesus. Jogues accepted Brother Goupil's vows in the name of the Society, and blessed him.

On the eighth day of their journey, they encountered a war party of two hundred Iroquois, who saluted their victorious countrymen with whoops of joy and volleys from their muskets. The captives were stripped and compelled to walk up a rocky hill between two lines of warriors, who beat the victims over the head and shoulders with clubs. Jogues was placed last in the line and was beaten with such fury that, drenched in blood, he fell stunned. They dragged him to the top of the hill.

Along with the other prisoners, French and Huron, Jogues was led to a platform where again they beat and stabbed him, mangled his fingers, and thrust burning fagots against his arms and thighs. A brave advanced toward him, brandishing a long knife. He seized the priest's nose and was about to cut it off. Jogues looked into the narrow slits of the Mohawk's eyes without shrinking. "Lord, take not only my nose," he prayed, "but also my head." The Indian hesitated and then lowered his knife.

Jogues knew that if his nose was amputated, he would be killed; it was the custom to put to death those badly mutilated. The same brave approached a second time, seized the priest's nose, and again raised his knife. Again he hesitated as he looked into the calm face of Jogues. He lowered the blade and walked away. Perhaps, thought Jogues, God still had work for him to do.

The Iroquois outdid themselves when they came to Eustace Ahatsistari, heaping worse cruelties upon him than even upon the other Hurons.

Finally the journey was resumed. Bleeding and famished, subsisting chiefly on wild berries, loaded with heavy packs, the captives dragged themselves along. It was thirteen days after the ambush, on the eve of the Assumption 1642, that they reached the goal of their agonized pilgrimage, Ossernenon, a palisaded town on a hill by the north bank of the Mohawk River.

The whoops of the escorting Iroquois brought forth a swarm of Indians, young and old, from the village. Quickly ranging themselves in a double line and clasping clubs or slender iron rods bought from the Dutch, they saluted the row of captives that passed between them with screeches and a hurricane of blows. One especially hard blow sent Jogues, who again brought up the rear, reeling to the ground. As the blows continued to rain down upon him, he staggered to his feet and gained the top of the hill.

Here the victims were led up to a platform. The three Frenchmen had fared the worst; their features were distorted and bleeding, Goupil's naked body livid with bruises from head to foot.

"Come," said a chief, waving a knife, "let us caress these Frenchmen."

The crowd surged up on the platform and beat and stabbed the prisoners. A sorcerer approached the priest and cried, "I hate this one most of all." With that, he commenced to gnaw his fingers. Next, he ordered a Christian Algonquin woman, a prisoner of the Mohawks, to saw off Jogues's left thumb with a jagged shell. She refused. The braves began to beat her and threatened to kill her. Trembling, she at last complied with reluctance.

When the thumb fell to the floor, Isaac picked it up and, as he later wrote, "I presented it to Thee, O my God, in remembrance of the sacrifices which for the last seven years I had offered on the altars of Thy Church and as an atonement for the want of love and reverence of which I have been guilty in touching Thy Sacred Body."

"Throw it down," whispered Couture, "or they will make you eat it."

Jogues hastily threw it away.

The Iroquois continued to torture the victims, cutting, stabbing, and burning until dusk fell. The prisoners then were placed in one of the houses, each of them stretched on his back, his limbs extended, his wrists and ankles bound fast to stakes driven into the earthen floor. It was time now for the children to amuse themselves. They placed live coals on the naked bodies. Sometimes the prisoners were able to shake off the coals. Like little demons, the youngsters chortled with glee when the victims were unable to dislodge the coals.

On the three following days, they were placed on the platform, where old and young, men and women, resumed their sport. At the end of that time, they were led to the adjoining villages of Andagarron and Tionontoguen, whose inhabitants regaled themselves on the prisoners.

In Tionontoguen the children were adept and shameless in devising ways of tormenting the victims bound to the floor. "What things," exclaims Jogues, "what sort of things did they not do to us thus bound? What did they not do to my Huron brothers? What things, what sort of things did they not attempt to do to me? But, again, I gave thanks to you, O my God, that always you have preserved me, your priest, pure from the impure hands of the savages."

In one house in this village, Jogues was hung up by the wrists so that his feet could not touch ground; for some fifteen minutes he so remained when suddenly a brave, moved by pity, shouldered his way through the crowd and cut the ropes. Jogues later learned that his rescuer was from another tribe and was visiting. The Indians' law of hospitality did not permit them to take reprisals upon their guest for his actions.

Also in Tionontoguen, while Jogues was still there, four fresh Huron captives were brought to the platform for the customary treatment. In spite of his pain and exhaustion, Jogues took the opportunity to convert them. An ear of green corn had been thrown to him for food, and he found a few raindrops clinging to the husk.

With these he baptized two of the Hurons. The other two he baptized soon after with water from a brook which the prisoners crossed on the way to another town.

Although the Indians had been enraged at Couture for killing one of their braves and had tortured him in return, they admired his pluck. Accordingly, he was adopted into the family of the chief whom he had slain and was assigned to live with them in Tionontoguen. There he was comparatively safe. Jogues and Goupil were given over to the chief who had captured them and were to be slaves in his cabin at Ossernenon. The three Huron chiefs were consigned to death by burning: Eustace at the capital town of Tionontoguen, the other two at Andagarron and Ossernenon, respectively. The remaining Hurons were given to various families, who might adopt, enslave, or kill them.

When he was back in Ossernenon, Jogues lost no opportunity to baptize dying infants, visit the sick, and, so far as he was able, win the Indians to Christianity. He was continually subjected to the ridicule of the sorcerers and to indignities from the populace. Life in his filthy cabin was an unending misery. Dogs and children crawled over his half-naked body, vermin swarmed over him, the cold nearly froze him, and the smoke was a constant irritation to his eyes. He lived in expectation of being burned at the stake or tomahawked by some young brave eager to show he had arrived at the warrior stage.

Meanwhile, the Dutch at Fort Orange learned on September 7 of the capture of Jogues and his companions. The commandant, Arendt van Corlear, accompanied by Jean Labatie and Jacob Jansen, came to ransom them. But word had reached Ossernenon that the war party who had tortured Jogues on Lake Champlain had been badly defeated by Montmagny at the fort that the governor had hurriedly erected at the mouth of the Richelieu. Furious, the Mohawks refused to exchange their prisoners, despite generous offers by the Dutch.

The mood of the Ossernenon Indians grew no less menacing. One day René Goupil, who occasionally taught the children to make the Sign of the Cross, made the sign on the forehead of the grandson of the Indian in whose lodge he was living. The old savage had once been told by the Dutch that the Sign of the Cross came from the Devil and would bring evil. Thinking that Goupil was bewitching the child, he enlisted the aid of two young braves to rid himself of so dangerous a guest.

Soon after, Jogues and Goupil were walking in the forest near the settlement; they were consoling themselves with prayer and steeling themselves for any trials that might befall them. On their return, they met two young braves, in whose faces they read trouble. The Indians followed them to the entrance of the village, where one of them drew a tomahawk from beneath his blanket and buried it in the skull of Goupil. René fell, uttering the name of Christ.

Jogues went down upon his knees and bowed his head, awaiting the blow, but he was ordered to rise and go to his cabin. Unheeding, Jogues knelt beside his dying friend and imparted absolution. He was just in time, for the braves took Goupil's lifeless body and dragged it through the town, amid hooting and rejoicing.

"Thus," wrote Jogues, "on the 29th of September, this angel of innocence and martyr of Jesus Christ was immolated in his thirty-fifth year for Him who had given His life for ransom. He had consecrated his heart and his soul to God, and his work and his life to the welfare of the poor Indians."

And so René Goupil was the first of the eight Jesuit Martyrs of North America to offer his life for the conversion of the Indians. The young physician had left the refinements of France to help humbly in the conversion of the wilderness inhabitants of the New World.

Jogues spent a sleepless night, heartbroken. Early the next day, he set out in search of René's body.

"Where are you going so fast?" demanded an old Indian. "Do you not see those fierce young braves who are watching to kill you?"

Jogues persisted in his intention. Seeing this, the old man requested another Indian to accompany him for protection. Jogues found the corpse in a nearby ravine, at the bottom of which flowed a stream. It was stripped naked and had been gnawed by dogs. To save it from further mutilation, he dragged it deeper into the water and covered it with stones, intending to return alone the following day and secretly bury it.

A storm broke that night. In the gray dawn, Jogues descended to the brink of the stream, which now was a turbid flood. The body was nowhere to be seen. Wading up to his waist in the cold current, Jogues sounded the bottom with his feet and with a stick. He searched among the rocks, the thickets, and the woods, but in vain. Crouched by the stream and in a voice broken by sobs and groans, he chanted the service of the dead.

Early that spring, he learned that the Indians, not the flood, had taken the body away; some Mohawk children told him it had been flung into a lonely spot lower down in the stream. Finally Jogues found the scattered bones, stripped clean by the foxes and the birds; the skull had been crushed in several places.

"I reverently kissed the hallowed remains," he says, and hid them in the earth[7] that I might one day, if such be the will of God, enrich with them a Christian and a holy ground. He deserves the

---

[7] The exact spot where Jogues buried the remains has never been discovered. It lies somewhere in the ravine at Auriesville, near the present Shrine of the Martyrs. Jogues's prayer that Goupil's remains might enrich a Christian and a holy ground has been fulfilled.

name of martyr not only because he has been murdered by the enemies of God and His Church while laboring in ardent charity for his neighbor, but most of all because he was killed for being at prayer and notably for making the Sign of the Cross."

Because Jogues was ordered by his superiors to write an account of his captivity, we have the vivid record of his life, which Francis Parkman has described as a living martyrdom. The priest was assigned the most degrading work and treated with greater contempt than the most despised squaw. He was made a beast of burden; heavy loads were placed on his bruised shoulders, and he was compelled to tramp fifty, seventy, a hundred miles after the Indians. They paraded their prize exhibit wherever they went. His wounds were gangrened, his bare feet left tracks of blood on snow and ice, the deerskin he wore was alive with vermin. He could well have said, with Saint Paul, "We are fools for Christ's sake. . . . We are made as the refuse of this world, the offscouring of all."[8]

Late that fall, a band of Mohawks set out on their annual deer hunt. Jogues was ordered to accompany them. Loaded down with burdens, half-famished, he trekked through the November cold and shared the Mohawks' mountain bivouacs. The game they caught was offered up to Areskoui, god of the chase, and eaten in his honor. Jogues, in consequence, would not taste the meat; to do so would be to participate in the worship of the demon. At night, when the kettle was slung and the savages were celebrating their success in the hunt, Jogues would crouch in a corner of the hut, shivering and starving in the midst of plenty.

His conduct mystified and annoyed the Mohawks, and if they returned in the evening with no game, they blamed it on the Blackrobe: he had offended Areskoui.

[8] 1 Cor. 4:10, 13.

Like a squaw, Jogues brought in firewood; he carried their loads; he was their slave in all things but one: when they mocked at his God, when they ordered him to worship theirs, the slave would assume a tone of authority and a steadfast attitude that astonished them.

At times Jogues would escape "this Babylon," as he called the camp site. Wandering off into the wilderness, he would recite the Rosary, repeat passages from the Scriptures, and read from *The Imitation of Christ*. In some lonely spot, he would carve the figure of the Cross into the trunk of a tree and there kneel in prayer for long periods.

"This living martyr," observes Parkman, "half-clad in shaggy furs, kneeling on the snow among the icicled rocks and beneath the gloomy pines, bowing in adoration before the emblem of the Faith in which was his only consolation and his only hope, is alike a theme for the pen and a subject for the pencil."

From Parkman's external portrayal, Jogues himself allows us to penetrate into his interior condition. "In this sadness," he recalls, "I had recourse to the help of the Scriptures, my accustomed refuge. The passages that I recalled in memory taught me how I should think of God in His infinite goodness. Although I was not upheld by sensible consolation, nevertheless I would know that 'the just man lives by faith.' I searched the Scriptures; I followed their streamlets, desiring, as it were, to quench my daily thirst. 'In the law of God I was meditating day and night,' and, indeed, unless the law of God had been my meditation, I would then perhaps have perished in my abjection."

In his forest retreats, Jogues would experience a desolation of soul that reflected the intellectual and spiritual isolation of his lot, intensified now by the loss of Goupil. Having no contact with his fellow countrymen, without the consolation of the Mass, without altar or chapel or any of the conventional aids to formal religious worship, physically beaten and mentally harassed, Jogues yet did not break down. So deep and unshakable was his supporting faith that he often cried out with Job, "Though he slay me, yet will I trust in Him."

Turning to God in his anguish, he heard an answering echo to his cry. "I heard, very distinctly," he relates, "a voice which condemned me for my anguish of soul, and which advised me to think of God only in His goodness, and to cast myself entirely upon Him. I heard, I repeat, those words which I understood to be from Saint Bernard writing to his monks: 'Serve God in that charity and love which cast out fear; such love does not regard merit.' These two counsels were given to me very opportunely, for my soul was being burdened down with an excessive fear." In that lonely shrine, he made, as well as he could, the spiritual exercises of the Jesuit's annual retreat.

The Mohawks were irritated by Jogues's refusal to participate in their rites to Areskoui. Loading him down with the head, neck, and the four quarters of a moose as payment to his master for Jogues's services, they sent him back to Ossernenon with some squaws and old men. His arms and legs, already frostbitten, now became scratched and bloody from the vines and underbrush through which he staggered. The nights he spent in a hollow of snow with no furs to protect him, although the Indians were returning with many.

They reached the gorge of a mountain stream, using for bridge a tree trunk thrown across. A pregnant squaw who was carrying a baby in a basket on her back slipped and fell into the swirling stream. She would have drowned had not Jogues plunged in and rescued her and the baby. A few days later the infant died, but not before the priest had baptized him.

The winter months dragged on. The cold split the bark on the trees. The Indians were huddled about their fires, buried day and night in a thick pall of smoke. Jogues crouched in a corner of the miserable hut, seeking protection from the piercing cold. His eyes were half-blinded by the smoke, and he pressed his face close to the earthen floor in an effort to breathe. When he could no longer endure it, he arose and went outside, only to be driven back by the sharp winds and the penetrating cold.

Through it all, nothing could discourage him from trying to improve the spiritual lot of the Indians. He could do little with the adults, who were hardened in their superstitious practices and their profligacy. But seldom did a baby die in Ossernenon without Baptism. He visited and instructed the Huron captives; when they were burned at the stake, he brought them the consolations of the Christian Faith. By the end of the year, Jogues was able to report seventy Baptisms, all of them accomplished on persons at the point of death.

Other consolations came to him. He was assigned to care for a man dying of a disease so loathsome that no Indian dared go near him. Jogues discovered that he was the brave who had beaten him on the torture platform and had torn out two of his fingernails. The stench from him was nauseating; Isaac gladly moved into the cabin and fed and nursed him until he passed away fifteen days later. It filled Jogues with exultation to be able to return love and kindness for hatred and cruelty.

One day the Indians, and Jogues with them, were passing through an Indian village, where they stopped and feasted. Jogues went from cabin to cabin to visit the sick. Entering one cabin, he heard his name called by a man dying in a dark corner.

"Ondessonk," he said, "don't you remember me?"

"No," replied the priest, racking his memory.

"I am the man who cut your bonds when you were hanging by the wrists in that hut of the Mohawks."

"Ah, yes!" said Jogues. "I remember you well, and I have prayed ever since that God would reward you."

Thereupon he instructed the man, who wanted to become a Christian. Jogues baptized him and was kneeling at his side when he died three hours later. The priest was certain that Divine Providence had guided his footsteps to that cabin; even in the condition of a slave to cruel masters, he rejoiced that he could be a channel of grace to human souls.

Jogues often made trips to the other Mohawk villages to take care of the spiritual needs of the Huron and Algonquin prisoners. These remained true to their new Faith and were further strengthened by the heroic example of the Jesuit.

In later years, Joseph Teondechoren, who had been ambushed with Jogues, said to Father Ragueneau, "Oh, how I love the crown, or Rosary, of the Holy Virgin! Never do I tire of reciting it; and she has granted to me all that I have asked of her when offering her this prayer. It was good Father Jogues who gave me this devotion when we were both captives in the country of the Iroquois. We often used to recite our Rosary together in the very streets of Anniene, the Mohawk village, without those infidels perceiving us."

Joseph's niece Theresa showed, even in captivity, that the religious training she had received from the Ursuline nuns at Quebec was not in vain. In the midst of profligacy, she remained unshaken in faith and in virtue. Having no beads, she used the tips of her fingers to recite the Rosary. Father Jogues's visits to her village seemed to her like visits from an angel.

Jogues had won the sympathy and respect of the elderly Indian couple in whose cabin he was now living. The squaw's brother was a chief, and she was not without influence. Often she showed little acts of kindness to Jogues. In March 1643, the couple set out with other families to their spring fishing grounds. They took with them their grandson and the priest. While they were fishing, Jogues went off one day into the woods and built a little cabin of bark in a grove of evergreens. He erected in it a cross, and used the cabin as an oratory. Here he spent long hours in prayer.

"How often," he recounts, "in those journeys and in that lonely retreat did we sit by the rivers of Babylon and weep, when we remembered thee, O Sion, not only exulting in Heaven, but even on earth praising thy God. How often, though in a strange land, have we sung the canticle of the Lord; and the woods and the mountains about resounded with the praises of their Creator, which never, from their creation, had they heard. How often on the stately trees of the forests did I carve the most Sacred Name of Jesus, so that, seeing it, the demons might take to flight and, hearing it, they might tremble with fear?"

A week after their arrival at the fishing grounds, some young braves arrived with the alarming news that a band of Algonquins was on the warpath nearby. The elderly Indian couple, with their grandson and the priest, were told to hasten back to the village. When they returned, they discovered that the story had been a ruse to get the Blackrobe back so that he could be tortured and burned to death. The rumor had reached Ossernenon that ten Mohawk warriors had been captured and killed by the Algonquins, allies of the French. Vengeance, therefore, was to be meted out to the Frenchman in their midst.

The torture and execution were set for the following day, Good Friday. That night Isaac Jogues prepared for the fate that had been hanging over him for almost a year. "The next day," he wrote, "which had closed the Savior's life, was now to end mine."

In the morning, a messenger rushed into the village. He reported that the ten warriors whom they thought had been killed had in reality joined the other Iroquois and were returning with twenty-two Abenaki prisoners. The whole village broke out in noisy jubilation. Men, women, and children rushed to the gates. Of the captives, six were men; the others were squaws and children of both sexes. The men were to be tortured and burned to death, the women and children adopted. Father Jogues did not know their language, but with the aid of an Algonquin woman he was able to instruct and baptize the captive warriors before they were led to death.

Jogues was once more reprieved.

A few weeks later, ambassadors from the Sokokis arrived at the village. The Sokokis were allies of the Iroquois and were at war with the French and the Algonquins. One of their great chiefs had been captured by the Algonquins and led in triumph to the French at Quebec. There, Governor Montmagny and the Jesuit Fathers gave the Algonquins many presents of great value and prevailed upon them to turn the distinguished prisoner over to the French. He was then freed by the French and was also loaded with presents. But before releasing him, the governor secured his promise that he would have his tribe intercede with their Mohawk friends for the release of Father Jogues.

The Mohawk chiefs assembled in council to consider the request. They accepted the presents that were proffered and agreed to release their Ondessonk and lead him back to the French. Satisfied, the Sokokis departed. But, contrary to the law and the custom of all the Indian nations, which obliges the tribe accepting presents to do what is asked of them, the Mohawks broke their promise. Indeed, as Jogues later learned, they had never had any intention of keeping it.

Jogues, Goupil, and Lalande

Early in May Father Jogues had his first chance to visit the Dutch at their Rensselaerswyck settlement, forty miles east of Ossernenon. He went under a strong guard of braves who were bent on trading furs and skins for Dutch merchandise.

Jogues was permitted to visit Arendt van Corlear, the commandant, and Jean Labatie, the Huguenot interpreter; both were trying to effect his release. Most congenial of all to Jogues, however, was the Dutch parson Dominie Megapolensis. He welcomed the Blackrobe as a brother in the Lord and had for him a most welcome present, Jogues's own breviary. One of the Iroquois had brought it to the Dutch for barter, and the dominie at once retrieved it. The kindly act of the minister deeply touched the Jesuit and made him rejoice to be with Christians once more.

The center of the Dutch settlement was Fort Orange, a miserable log structure that stood within the limits of the present city of Albany. There were several houses and a small church that served also as the parson's dwelling. Scattered along the Hudson River, above and below the fort, were about thirty houses built of boards and roofed with thatch. The hundred-odd inhabitants were mostly Dutch peasants, tenants of the patroon, or lord of the manor, Van Rensselaer.

The Dutch got on well with the Indians and sometimes intermarried with them. They exchanged guns, knives, kettles, axes, and beads for the furs of the Indians, and the trade was a profitable one. The Dutch burghers pleaded with the Mohawks and offered them large ransoms to surrender Father Jogues, but the Indians refused. Such action, they alleged, could be taken only by the great council of the nation. Very probably, they said, he would be released to the French governor during the summer.

During this visit with the Dutch, Jogues secured pen, ink, and writing paper. For some time he had been observing preparations by the Iroquois to attack the French and their Indian allies, and he was anxious to get word to Montmagny. Accordingly be wrote the governor a letter in French, Latin, and Huron, which, if it fell into enemy hands, would be incomprehensible. The letter warned of the Iroquois designs to capture as many French as possible and to exterminate the Huron nation. No consideration of him or of his safety, it went on, must deter them from taking effective measures to thwart the plan of the Indians.

Jogues gave the letter into the care of the renegade Huron who had become a Mohawk chief, the same who had led the flotilla that ambushed Jogues and his party on their journey from Quebec to Huronia. Jogues distrusted the man, but felt it necessary to use the most likely means of warning the French in time. He was to learn soon afterward of the consequences of his efforts.

After a few days with the Dutch, the Mohawks returned to Ossernenon, taking Jogues with them. Shortly after their return, twelve braves marched proudly into the village, on May 24, with a collection of prisoners.

"On Pentecost," writes Jogues, "they brought in new prisoners, three women with their little children. The men were killed near the French settlement. The three women and children were led into the village, entirely naked, without even loin cloths. They were horribly beaten with clubs and their thumbs were cut off. One of them (and this was an act never done before) was burned all over her body and was then thrown into a roaring funeral pyre. Then I was a witness to something new, something worthy of note. When this woman was being tortured, at every burn which the Mohawks inflicted on her by applying lighted torches to various parts of her body, an old man, in a strong and vigorous voice, cried out these words: 'Great god Areskoui, we offer thee this victim whom we burn for thee, that thou mayst eat of her flesh and that thou mayst always from now on make us victors over our enemies.' Her body was cut into pieces, and these were carried to the various villages, where they were eaten.

"The reason," he proceeds to explain, "was this: About the middle of winter, the Mohawks grieved that they had abstained from eating the flesh of some of their prisoners. In a solemn sacrifice they had offered two bears to their divinity and had addressed him in these words: 'Great god Areskoui, justly dost thou punish us, since now for a long time thou hast not permitted us to take any of our enemies captive. We have sinned against thee, because we did not eat the last captives thrown by thee into our hands. But if, in the future, we capture any Algonquins, we swear to you that we will devour them in the same way that we are now about to eat these two bears.' They kept their pledge."

Isaac Jogues baptized this woman while she was burning on the pyre. He had not been able to do it before, when he was offering a drink to her parched lips. No horror which the Indians were able to perpetrate deterred the priest from performing his ministry.

~

Chapter 4

It was summer, and the couple with whom Jogues was living were about to set out with the seasonal fishing party. He was to accompany them. They would spend a few days at the Dutch settlement to trade, and the elderly squaw, who felt toward Jogues the fondness of an aunt, gave him to understand that if he wished to escape with the aid of the Dutch, she would not hinder him in any way.

Isaac carefully weighed the pros and cons of escape and ended by rejecting it. "Although in all possibility," he writes, "I could escape either through the Europeans or through other savages living around us, if I should wish it, I decided to live on this cross on which our Lord had fixed me in company with Himself, and to die with His grace helping me. For who would be able to give solace to the French captives if I were absent? Who could absolve them after their confessions? Who could remind the baptized Hurons of their duty? Who could instruct the prisoners who were being constantly brought in? Who could baptize them when they were dying and strengthen them in their torments? Who could pour the sacred waters on the heads of the children? Who look after the salvation of the adults who were dying, and after the instruction of those in good health? Indeed, I believe that it happened not without a singular providence of the divine goodness, that I should have fallen into the hands of these very savages."

Having come to his decision, Jogues hid his breviary and the packet containing the Huron *Relation* and the letters he had salvaged from the Mohawks. With him, he took two small books, *The Imitation of Christ* and *The Little Office of the Blessed Virgin*.

At Rensselaerswyck the Dutch treated him most hospitably. They invited him to their homes and to their taverns, there to enjoy a stein of beer, a glass of gin, or a cup of mulled wine.

"It is good for your health," they urged, "and it will raise your spirits."

Isaac thanked them politely and declined. He wished to set a good example for the Indians, who so quickly became intoxicated and behaved like wild beasts. Often he had spoken to them of the evils flowing from their addiction to firewater, and he felt it incumbent upon him now to back his words by example.

Jogues did enjoy the company of the Dutch, however, and particularly of the dominie. With him, he was able to engage in intellectual conversation, for which he was literally famished.

He was most anxious, while in Rensselaerswyck, to report to his superior in France concerning his long captivity. He was able to steal away from the Indians for varying intervals, and he wrote to Father Jean Filleau, the Jesuit Provincial in France:

When I sat down to write to your Reverence, the first doubt that came to me was whether I should write in Latin or in French, since I have almost forgotten both languages after so long a disuse of them. . . . The very great charity of your Reverence . . . will pardon me if there be some fault against the rules of decorum or language, for they will have been committed by a man who has lived for eight years after the manner and even in the appearance and dress of the savages.

Then, despite his want of practice in Latin, despite his maimed fingers, he proceeded to detail in more than thirty pages of fine script his many and varied experiences during the previous fourteen months. Humility, zeal, self-effacement, and submission to God's will sounded throughout the recital.

While Jogues was with the Dutch, some braves came in from Ossernenon. Through them he heard the repercussions of the warning letter he had sent to the French. The Huron-turned-Mohawk had presented the letter to the French at their recently built fort at the mouth of the River Richelieu. By so doing, he thought to ingratiate himself and his party with the French so that the Mohawks might the more effectively carry out their treachery.

The commander of the post read the letter and, with no effort to disguise the nature of the message and so spare Jogues, turned his cannon upon the waiting Indians. They fled in dismay, leaving their baggage and some of their guns. Wild with anger, they hastened to Ossernenon to wreak their vengeance upon the Blackrobe.

Hearing this, Jogues knew that torture and death at the stake were plainly waiting for him. The Dutch urged him to escape. A small Dutch vessel, nearly ready to sail, lay in the Hudson opposite the settlement.

"Here is your chance," said Van Corlear, the commandant. "Slip into that vessel and hide. It is going to Virginia first, and from there it will take you to Bordeaux or La Rochelle, where it is going to land."

"But," objected the priest, "the Indians may suspect that you and your friends have aided in my escape and vent their wrath upon you."

"No, we can manage that all right," replied Van Corlear. "It would be death, yes, plain suicide for you to return to Ossernenon."

"Thanks, indeed," said Isaac, "for your kindness. I shall never forget it. Let me pray over the matter tonight and ask God to guide me. My life is of little moment. I want only to choose that course which will enable me to do most for souls and for the winning of the Indians to Christ."

He passed the night in prayer, asking God to allow no self-love to enter the making of his decision. In the course of the night, he came to see, more and more clearly, that his immediate usefulness as a spiritual shepherd to the Indians had come to an end. If he returned to Ossernenon, he would almost certainly be burned to death; even if he were not executed, the Indians would no longer allow him the freedom necessary to visit the Christian captives or to baptize the dying. Furthermore, Couture had often urged him to escape, promising that he would follow, whereas if Jogues did not escape, Couture would remain where he was.

Isaac Jogues had spent fourteen months in Gethsemane, and the sojourn had many times threatened to end at Calvary. Now God seemed to be opening the door for him. Why should he close it? His decision was made. He would escape. By so doing, he could continue to serve God and perhaps find some new way to advance His Kingdom in the New World.

The Dutch had been dumbfounded that he had not grasped at the chance that was offered to him; now they were delighted when he told them of his decision. A boat, they told him, would be left for him on the shore. He must watch his chance and escape in it to the waiting ship, whose captain had sworn to protect him.

Isaac and his Mohawk masters were lodged together in a large building that belonged to a prosperous Dutch farmer married to a Mohawk squaw. It was about one hundred feet long and had no partitions of any kind. At one end were the horses, cattle, and chickens. At the other end slept the farmer and his wife and children. The Indians lay on the floor in the middle.

Early in the night, under cover of perfect darkness, Jogues crept out softly, picking his way among the prostrate figures. He saw that a picket fence extended around the farmyard and the building. While he was reconnoitering, a huge watchdog came charging upon him and bit him severely in the leg. The Dutchman rushed out, followed by the Indians, to find the cause of the commotion. The farmer led the priest back into the barn by the light of a candle and applied to the wounds the only remedy he knew, hair from the mastiff. Then he wrapped a rag around the injured leg.

The angered Redskins barred the door more securely and made Ondessonk lie down between two of the braves. Still trembling from his encounter with the dog, stabbed by pain from the wound, and wedged in between two of the Indians, Isaac spent a sleepless night, fearful that his plans had been thwarted. A dull pain of frustration seized him.

When the first flush of dawn was breaking through the crevices, Jogues heard a door creak. Half-raising himself, he discerned a servant who had come with a lantern to begin his round of chores. It was now or never. Wriggling out from between the sleeping guards, he stuffed into his blouse his two precious books, The Imitation and The Little Office, put his small wooden cross into his pocket, and tiptoed to the door. By signs, he asked the servant to tie up the dogs. Like all the Dutch, the servant was eager to see Jogues make his escape. Quieting the dogs, he silently led the way out and showed him the path to the river, about half a mile away.

Fevered with excitement, Jogues thanked him and hurried, running and limping, along the narrow path. This ran through a marshy stretch where reeds and thorns scratched his naked legs.

Finally he reached the shore where the rowboat awaited him. But the tide had receded several feet, and the boat was stuck fast. Jogues pushed and tugged, but it would not budge. He hallooed to the ship, but none of the crew was astir. Louder he shouted, but no one appeared.

Jogues grew frantic. The Mohawks would be stirring any moment now, and he would be in full view of them. Praying to God for help, he gripped the prow and tugged with all his might. It gave a few inches in the mire. Again he pulled, and again. It moved a little, then more and more. He was breathing heavily now and almost fainting from exhaustion. But with the courage of desperation he gave a last superhuman pull and saw the boat ease into the water.

"Thanks be to God!" he cried aloud.

He jumped in and rowed out to the vessel, climbed the rope ladder, and scrambled onto the deck. The captain and crew greeted him heartily. They hid him in the bottom of the hold and placed a large box over the hatchway.

When the Indians awoke and found that Ondessonk was gone, they were infuriated. They ran screaming through the streets; they searched the woods and the houses of the Dutch. They were in an angry mood and accused the Dutch of conniving in his escape. They made menacing threats, and Van Corlear could not placate them. He offered them three hundred guldens, which they spurned. They wanted their prize captive back, and they threatened reprisals — they might slaughter the burghers' cattle, or worse.

Alarmed, Van Corlear and his council decided that in such a crisis they could not allow Jogues to sail away. They would bring him back and conceal him until the danger was past. Dominie Megapolensis was commissioned to persuade him to return.

Jogues, Goupil, and Lalande

Out in the vessel's dark hold, Isaac Jogues was suffering tortures from the inflamed wound. Infection had set in, and the leg was swelling badly. He was almost suffocating in his stuffy, stinking, underwater prison. He could not suppress the hope for escape, yet his prayer even now was "that I might not withdraw from His wishes . . . that He might detain me in the country of those infidels if He did not approve my escape and flight."

When Dominie Megapolensis and the commandant of the fort came aboard, he was brought up on deck. He listened calmly while the dominie set forth the proposal of the Dutch: they did not want to surrender him, but to have him at hand — just in case the Indians went on a rampage.

The captain of the vessel roundly denounced the proposal as a piece of abject cowardice and betrayal. He had sworn that once the priest had set foot on his vessel, he would be safe. Jogues, he pointed out, had put his life in greater jeopardy by trusting their joint promises; to take him ashore would surely expose him to greater danger of discovery, even if the burghers did not hand him over to the Indians.

Deeply touched by the manly indignation and loyalty of the sea captain, Jogues explained that he would not think of imperiling the Dutch to save his own life. He was willing to sacrifice himself at any time rather than have others suffer in property or limb. He told the captain he gladly released him from his pledge.

Then, turning to the dominie and the commandant, he said, "Gentlemen, I most assuredly do not desire that, on any account, any harm whatsoever should happen to your cattle, and much more, any harm to your persons. The thought that I have had of freeing myself from the hands of the Iroquois and escaping death was suggested, first of all, by you. And so, since you now feel, or think, as you do about my escape, I relinquish my desire. I am quite prepared to give myself up to the Iroquois again. Have no doubt about that."

When he had finished his brave little speech, he sagged to the floor in a dead faint. He had been without sleep for four nights and had had scarcely any food; he had become sickened by the stench and stuffiness of the hold and poisoned by the leg wound, which now was gangrened. His last ounce of nervous energy was drained by the excitement of this new crisis, and he had crumpled like a bird exhausted in a storm. When he came to, he arose and told them he was ready to leave for shore.

Wrongly attributing his swooning to fear, the dominie explained at careful length that they would not abandon him to the Mohawks, whose angry mood would surely pass away; only in the unlikely event that the Indians became truly violent would the Dutch consider handing him over. Isaac heard him through patiently and repeated that he was quite willing to return to Rensselaerswyck and even to Ossernenon. "In all these proceedings," Jogues later reported, "I might have urged some arguments in my favor. But it was not for me to speak in my own behalf; rather it was for me to follow the orders of these others."

A little later, exhausted and feverish, Isaac Jogues lay hidden in the commandant's house. The Dutch surgeon was seriously considering the necessity of amputating Jogues's leg to save his life.

Jogues wrote a long letter on August 30, 1643, to Father Charles Lalemant, then in France, narrating the details of the last few days. In concluding the letter, he says, "Here, then, I remain a voluntary prisoner in the house of the commandant, from which I am writing to you the present letter. If you ask my thoughts in all these adventures, I will tell you, first, that the ship which had sought to save my life sailed without me. Secondly, if our Lord does not protect me in a manner almost miraculous, the savages will discover me, for they come and go here at every moment. If ever they suspect that I have not gone away, I must necessarily be returned to their hands. Now, if they were so enraged against me before my flight, what treatment will they inflict on me when I fall again under their power? I shall not die a common death; the fire, their anger, and the cruelties they will invent will actually tear away my life. God be blessed forever! We are always in the bosom of His divine and ever adorable Providence. . . . Pray for these poor nations that burn and devour one another, that at last they may come to the knowledge of their Creator in order to render to Him the tribute of their love. I do not forget you; my captivity cannot fetter my memory."

A day or two later, the commandant thought it expedient to remove Jogues from the fort to the house of the sutler. This trader was a crotchety character, anything but eager to take in his new guest. From the storeroom of his frame house a ladder led up to the attic; here was a large room in which was stored some of his merchandise. A small corner under the ridgepole was partitioned off by a circular wall of loosely placed, wide boards. Into this compartment was brought Isaac Jogues.

The slanting roof was so low that one could stand upright in the center only. It was a veritable oven during the day, for there was only a tiny window under the gable to ventilate it. When it rained heavily, the water poured through the thatch and flooded the garret. Jogues's bed was the planks of the floor.

Worse than the physical discomforts was the constant danger of being discovered. The Mohawks swarmed inside the store and out. Jogues could hear their guttural voices in the courtyard just below. If he walked about, they could hear the creaking downstairs in the store. And when the sun shone in at a particular angle, his body cast a shadow against the partition that could readily be seen.

Sometimes the merchant would bring the Indians up the ladder to the open part of the attic, where they might examine the merchandise. Only the thin board partition separated them from the refugee, who could hear their footsteps, their conversation, and their very breathing. On occasion he remained crouched for a period of four hours, fearing they would notice his shadow if he made the slightest movement.

The merchant gave him barely enough food to keep him alive, and Jogues suffered acutely from lack of drinking water. When the merchant finished making lye every two weeks, he would give the tub a casual washing, carry it to the loft, and fill it with water for the priest. After a few days, the stifling heat and the particles of lye adhering to the sides of the tub combined to make the water unfit to drink. When his mouth and throat became intensely parched, Jogues had no alternative but to drink the fetid water, though. It made him deathly ill and caused him painful cramps.

His only visitor was the dominie, who did not know when the danger from the Indians would end or when Isaac could be released. On one of his visits, he asked Jogues how he was being treated. The priest replied that he was content, that he was accustomed to suffering; but he did mention that he received very little to eat. The dominie knowingly shook his head.

"I rather suspected that," he said. "This old man is a terrible miser, and doubtless he has been keeping for himself most of the provisions sent for you."

Thereafter Isaac fared better. Hot August faded with agonizing slowness into September, and still there came no sign of release. He wondered whether the door of his prison ever would open. In his tight little attic cell, Jogues read his two books and spent long periods in prayer and meditation. "Only God and His saints," wrote Father Lalemant, "were his company. Stripped of all earthly things, he achieved ever closer union with God and drew his strength from Him."

~

In France, word of Isaac Jogues's captivity had reached the queen regent, Anne of Austria. She appealed to the Netherlands government to take measures toward his speedy release. Her request was transmitted by the states-general to Director-General Kieft at New Amsterdam. Kieft sent a peremptory command to the director and commandant at Fort Orange to bring the Jesuit missionary down to Fort Amsterdam at the earliest possible moment.

The order reached Rensselaerswyck at about the time when a delegation of Mohawk chiefs had arrived to hold council with the Dutch. Van Corlear tried to beguile them in the first council; then he endeavored to bribe them with a generous ransom. When they remained obdurate, he changed his tactics: he told them bluntly that he had taken Ondessonk under his protection. If they refused his gift of three hundred guldens, the Dutch would refuse to trade with them further.

After much haggling and unending flowery speeches, the chiefs accepted the gift and professed to be consoled over the loss of the Jesuit.

It was the last week of September, and under cover of darkness, Jogues was smuggled from the merchant's garret to a sloop that was to sail in the morning. Here, after six weeks of solitary confinement, Jogues drew his first breath of freedom. He was happy with his unaccustomed security — above all because he now could plan how to return later on and again devote his energies to the eternal welfare of the natives of the New World. Christ would yet reign in their hearts, and His gospel of mercy and love would become the law of all the nations throughout the broad wilderness.

The Dutch sailors treated him with the greatest kindness and respect. His courage and self-effacement had won them. "Halfway down the Hudson," he relates, "they celebrated my release by stopping at an island which they called by my name, and gave evidence of their pleasure by the discharge of cannon and the uncorking of bottles."[9]

In six days they reached Manhattan. The governor gave him an honorable reception and seated him next to the dominie. The ragged attire he had been wearing had been replaced with new clothing. The presence of a priest on Manhattan Island, the first ever to put foot there, caused a great stir among the colonists. Bearing the marks of his terrible sufferings, he was regarded with awe and treated with unending kindliness. One young man knelt at his feet and raised the mangled hands of the priest to his lips.

"Martyr of Jesus Christ!" he exclaimed. "Martyr of Christ!"

"Are you a Catholic?" asked Jogues, rather startled.

"No, I am a Lutheran," he replied, "but I recognize you as one who has suffered for the Master."

Jogues spent a month among his Dutch friends. Looking about him at leisure, he saw a dilapidated fort, containing a garrison of sixty soldiers. He saw the stone church, the director-general's house, the barracks, the stone houses. Numbers of small dwellings nearby were occupied mostly by mechanics and workmen. The houses of the other colonists were scattered about the island and on the neighboring shores. The settlers were of various faiths and nationalities, chiefly Dutch Calvinists.

---

[9] What island was this, christened in so cordial a fashion? The only one that would fit the description is that now known as Esopus Island. It lies in the center of the river and is now within the corporate limits of Ulster County, New York.

During this time, a bloody feud was going on with the Indians of that region. Eighty Redskins were reported killed in one encounter, sixteen hundred in another; some forty of the Dutch lost their lives on the outlying farms, and many houses and barns were burned.

A small trading vessel was to sail for the Netherlands on November 5, and the commander-general gave Jogues free passage. The voyage was stormy. Jogues slept on the bare deck or on a coil of rope, shivering from the cold and often drenched by the waves that broke over the lugger's side. At last the vessel entered the harbor of Falmouth in Cornwall, hotly pursued by some of Cromwell's ships; the rebellion against Charles I was in progress at the time.

The crew went ashore for a carouse, leaving the missionary alone on the deck. A small vessel pulled alongside, and a band of marauders boarded her and robbed her of everything valuable. At the point of a pistol they relieved Jogues of his hat and coat. Soon after, a compassionate Frenchman whom he met on the shore secured passage for him across the Channel on a small coaling vessel.

The captain told Father Jogues that they would reach the islands off Finisterre early the next morning. That would be Christmas, and there would be Masses in the churches of the Breton fishing villages. Seventeen months had passed since the priest had said his last Mass, seventeen months since his confession to Father Buteux at Three Rivers. Famished for Mass and for the Holy Eucharist, Jogues mustered up courage to ask the captain if he would put him ashore at one of the villages so that he could assist at Mass. The captain agreed to do so if the weather held fair.

As the collier splashed through the choppy waters, Isaac Jogues huddled under a shelter on deck and examined his conscience. He had lived in an environment of sin; immorality had been open and flagrant and all about him. Had he at any time harbored impure thoughts? He had been abused, insulted, tortured, almost executed. Did he entertain hatred or feelings of revenge? At last the litany of possible sins gave way to memories of the little chapel at Sainte Marie, where he had celebrated Christmas Mass for his Huron flock. Tomorrow would be another Christmas, and he could hardly believe that he was to celebrate it in France; he was feverish with excitement.

The night slowly faded, and the French coast was visible. The ship was making for a point of land halfway between Brest and St. Paul de Léon. A rowboat was let down, and in a few minutes Father Jogues stepped on the shore of France for the first time in seven years.

~

Isaac Jogues hurried to a little stone house across the sand. Two men were standing in the doorway. They watched with curiosity as the odd-looking figure in the battered sailor's cap and the ragged overcoat much too large for him walked toward them. They took him to be an Irish refugee: many such had landed on the shores of Brittany the past few years, for bloody persecution of Catholics was raging in Ireland and England.

To their surprise, he addressed them in French, inquiring if there was a church nearby where he might hear Mass. The maimed condition of his hands would preclude his celebrating the Sacrifice himself. Yes, up the road a bit, they said, was a monastery of the Récollets where Mass would be said shortly. But he should look more decent, they thought, going to church. They put a better-looking cap on his head and tied a scarf around his neck, and they made him promise to return for breakfast.

The refugee hurried up the road that early Christmas morning. His heart was beating fast, and his soul sang *Noël! Noël!*,

Venite Adoremus, and the other Christmas hymns he had sung as a little boy. *Noël,* the day that Christ was born! France and Christmas! Why, surely it was too good to be true!

He knelt before a gray-robed priest, made his confession, and heard the words of absolution. He joined the fisherfolk on the flagged floor near the altar. The candles blazing, the priest in white vestments, the choir singing the old sweet hymns, the words of the Mass — a lump grew in his throat, and his eyes were moist. Now he was kneeling at the Communion rail. He felt the sacred Host, the Body of Christ, upon his tongue. He bent low in adoration. One devout Communion, he recalled, was worth all the trouble of a lifetime. His head cleared. "It seemed to me," he relates, "that it was at this moment that I began to live once more. It was then that I tasted the sweetness of my deliverance."

When he came back to the fisherman's cottage, they noticed the mutilated hands, the maimed fingers. Some of these were mere stumps, some had no fingernails; the left thumb was missing entirely. They looked more closely now at the sunken cheeks, the roughened skin, the hair prematurely gray. Who was this stranger?

When Isaac Jogues uncovered his identity, there were no bounds to their veneration and kindness. Their two little daughters gathered their savings — a few pennies — and put them into his hands. Deeply touched, and not wishing to hurt their feelings or to belittle their gift, he put the coins in his pocket, thanked them from the bottom of his heart, and blessed them.

A trader of Rennes brought a horse to the door and offered the use of it to the missionary to carry him to the Jesuit college in that city. Jogues gratefully accepted. He mounted the horse and, together with the trader, set out on the journey of some two hundred miles along the winding trails of the Côte du Nord.

He arrived early in the morning of January 5, 1644. He knocked at the door of the college; the porter opened it and beheld a man wearing a peasant hat and clothing little better than a tramp's. The stranger asked to see the rector. The rector, he was informed, was in the sacristy preparing to say Mass. The caller begged him to say that a man was at the door with news from Canada.

The Canadian missions were then uppermost in the minds of the French Catholics, especially of the Jesuits. The rector put aside the vestments and hurried to the parlor.

Not disclosing his identity, Isaac handed him a letter from the Dutch director-general, attesting his good character. But the rector was eager for more important news. Without reading the letter, he asked about the missions in Canada and if he knew Father Jogues.

"I know him very well."

"The Iroquois have taken him," continued the rector. "Is he dead? Have they murdered him?"

"No, he is alive and at liberty . . . and it is he who speaks to you!"

He fell on his knees and asked his superior's blessing.

There was great joy that day among the Jesuits at Rennes. They drank in the story of Isaac's captivity and his escape from the Indians. They learned of the gallant struggle of their fellow Jesuit to evangelize the savages of the American forest. They learned of the missions and of the colonists in New France.

Father Jogues quickly became a center of curiosity and of reverent interest to all France. Expressions of homage and admiration poured in upon him from every quarter. He was summoned to Paris by the queen, Anne of Austria, who wished to see him. When the tortured slave of the Mohawks was conducted into the presence of her majesty, surrounded by a host of the nobility, he concealed his hands in the folds of his cloak. He was asked to tell his adventures among the frightful barbarians of the American forests. Modestly, he related some of the high points of his captivity and of his work among the Hurons and the Iroquois. He answered their many questions with quiet humility.

When he was obliged to show his mutilated hands, to describe how the fingernails had been pulled out and the fingers chewed and burned and the thumb sawed off with a shell, the queen descended from the throne. Taking his hands in hers, and with tears streaming down her cheeks, she devoutly kissed the tormented fingers. "People write romances for us," she exclaimed, "but was there ever such a romance as this?"

To Isaac Jogues, public exhibitions of this character were equal to the tortures of the Iroquois. He shied away from the esteem and passionate interest of the highborn and the lowly. He became quite sensitive to references to his sufferings, and visitors were cautioned not to mention them. His only delight was to be a "fool for Christ's sake," "the offscouring of all," not to occupy the limelight and receive the plaudits of the multitude.

Jogues's supreme grief was that he would certainly be debarred forever from saying Mass. His left thumb had been sawed off at the root, and the index finger was only a stub; so shortened and distorted were the thumb and index finger of the right hand that he could not hold the Host in the prescribed manner. The superior general of the Society of Jesus sent a petition, accompanied by letters royal from Queen Anne and her council, to the Holy See to secure a dispensation from the canonical requirements.

Pope Urban was deeply moved by the story of Father Jogues's captivity and torture, and immediately granted the dispensation. "*Indignum esset Christi martyrem Christi non bibere sanguinem,*" he exclaimed: "It would be shameful that a martyr of Christ be not allowed to drink the Blood of Christ."

Father Jogues was raised to the seventh heaven. It had been twenty months since he had ascended the altar on August 1 to celebrate, with a prophetic fitness not then realized, the Mass of St. Peter in Chains. Now he was to enjoy again the highest privilege of the priesthood. With sentiments of throbbing joy and devotion akin, perhaps, to those experienced at his first Mass, Father Isaac Jogues ascended the altar of God to offer the Divine Oblation.

~

Chapter 5

Isaac Jogues wanted to escape the honors and the homage. The Indian missions were in his blood, and he pined for the copper-colored children of the wilderness. He desired particularly to win the fierce Iroquois to Christ, to prove to them that love triumphs over hatred. Knowing how desperately undermanned the missions were, he yearned like a dedicated soldier to be back to his post of duty.

He petitioned his superiors to allow him to return, and to his indescribable joy, the request was granted.

Toward the end of April 1644, he was on his way, stopping at Orléans to visit his mother. How different he looked to her from the youth she had held in her arms eight years before! Tenderly she ran her fingers over the scars on his face and neck and arms, and fondled his mutilated hands. She was proud of this son who had earned the gratitude of all France and of the Church, but her pride was pierced with sadness to learn that Isaac was headed back to the American missions. She knew that as he had heeded the voice of God eight years ago, so, now, the voice was calling him again, and it would be futile to pit her wishes against His.

Isaac's parting joy was to say Mass in his mother's presence and to place the Host upon her tongue. But well they both knew that this might be their last time together. "Adieu till we meet again," she said, wiping a tear from her eye, "though it may not be until we meet in Heaven."

He sailed from La Rochelle in the first week of May. On the vessel he found a company of soldiers who were to reinforce the French in the New World, even as he was to reinforce the mission. The passage was stormy, and the crew mutinied. Only the diplomatic intervention of Father Jogues quieted the sailors and prevented them from throwing the captain overboard.

The vessel nosed into Quebec late in June, and Isaac was welcomed heartily. The joy of reunion was tarnished for Jogues when he learned that the Iroquois were slaughtering the Hurons and the Algonquins, apparently bent on exterminating them. And they were attacking the French all along the St. Lawrence. At Montreal, where a settlement had been planted two summers before, Paul de Maisonneuve was putting up a vigorous defense behind the beleaguered stockades. And to Montreal Jogues was sent to minister to the sick and dying and to bolster the courage of the defenders.

The Indians at last requested a parley, and a conference was called to take place at Three Rivers on July 12, 1645, in an effort to establish peace. To assist in the conference, Jogues paddled down the St. Lawrence in his canoe. He was delighted to meet William Couture, who had come with the Mohawks as an envoy.

The council convened in a great tent in the courtyard of the fort. Governor Montmagny occupied the seat of honor. On his right was the commandant of Three Rivers; on his left sat the Jesuits Vimont, Le Jeune, and Jogues. In the center, facing the governor, were the Iroquois deputies, and back of them were the Algonquins,

Montagnais, and Attikameges. The Hurons and the French were on either side.

Indian oratory flowed, and there was much interchange of presents. All present professed willingness to bury the hatchet and live in peace and friendship.

The council decided to send an ambassador to the Mohawks to obtain that tribe's assent to the mutual concessions made by the deputies present. With the exception of Couture, no white man understood their language and character as well as Isaac Jogues, and Isaac was chosen for this difficult and perilous task. His assignment was both political and religious; in addition to bearing gifts, wampum belts, and messages from the governor, and seeking their acquiescence in the treaty, he was to found a new mission. (Prophetically, it was to be christened The Mission of the Martyrs.)

Jogues spent long periods in prayer, night and day, before the Blessed Sacrament. He wanted to be spiritually well-armed to meet the contingencies of his new assignment; although his official character of ambassador would protect him, the Iroquois would regard him primarily as a Blackrobe, with unpredictable consequences. An Algonquin convert, realizing this and being fearful for Jogues's safety, offered him this counsel: "Say nothing about the Faith at first, for there is nothing so repulsive in the beginning as our doctrine, which seems to destroy everything we hold dear; and as your long cassock preaches as well as your lips, you had better put on a short coat."

Jogues accordingly exchanged the uniform of Loyola for the civilian's doublet and hose. His superior, Father Jerome Lalemant, observed, "One should be all things to all men that one may gain them to Jesus Christ."

The conference at Three Rivers had been so protracted, and the preparations for Jogues's role of ambassador for the French and for the missions required such care, that it was not until May 16, 1646 that he was ready to set forth, almost two years after his arrival at Montreal. He left with the governor's engineer, Jean Bourdon, two Algonquins bearing gifts to confirm the peace, and four Mohawks to guide and escort the party. He traveled the River Richelieu and the length of Lake Champlain, continuing on to the foot of Lake George.

He had crossed the clear waters of Lake George three summers before, but then had been in no condition to observe its beauty. Now he marveled at the sparkling waters and the countless garden-like islands. The thought came to him that he would like to give it a name that would correspond with its loveliness. Recalling that this was the eve of Corpus Christi, he named it the Lake of the Blessed Sacrament. It was known by that name until a century later, when an ambitious Irish landowner, Sir William Johnson, sought to gain favor with the dull Hanoverian King and changed it to Lake George.

Jogues crossed on foot to a fishing settlement of the Mohawks, at a place now known as Beaver Dam. There, to his delight, he met Theresa, Joseph Teondechoren's niece, who had been captured with him by the Mohawks. She had married a warrior of the tribe and remained as staunch in the Faith as on the day she left the Ursuline convent in Quebec. Her joy in encountering Father Jogues can readily be imagined, and before they parted, he told her that his first care would be to purchase her freedom.[10]

Borrowing canoes at the fishing station, Jogues and his party descended to Fort Orange, where Isaac met the Dutch friends to whom he owed his life. He reimbursed them the three hundred

[10]It was promised but not secured. Theresa never reached her own country.

guldens they had paid for his ransom and passed a few pleasant days in their company.

On June 5, three weeks after his departure from Montreal, Jogues came to Ossernenon, the place of his long captivity. Crowds from the neighboring villages gathered to gaze with awe upon the man they had known as a slave, abused and scorned, but who now appeared among them as the ambassador of a great power that they were now in a mood to propitiate.

A council was held, and Ondessonk was the principal speaker. He assured his ancient tormenters that "the council fires lighted at Three Rivers would never be extinguished." He offered them the governor's gifts and the wampum belts, and announced to them the council's messages of peace. "Here," he said, "are five thousand beads of wampum to break the fetters of the young Frenchmen you hold as captives, and five thousand more for Theresa, that they may be set free."'

Grunts of approval issued from the throats of the assembled braves. The arrangements made at Three Rivers were approved, and the peace treaty on which the French colonial authorities, the Blackrobes, the Algonquins, and the Hurons had labored so earnestly was acquiesced in. The members of the Wolf clan, which had opposed Jogues's execution when he was a Mohawk captive, were now particularly friendly toward him. They said, "You shall always have among us a mat to rest upon and a fire to warm you."

Less enthusiasm was manifested when the Algonquin deputies addressed the assemblage; indeed, the gifts to them were received coldly. The old fires of hatred, kept aflame by long traditions of mutual atrocities, burned fiercely under the veneer of peace and were not to be extinguished overnight.

There were several Onondagas present, and Jogues made an earnest and successful bid for their friendship. He presented them with coveted gifts and secured from them a promise to receive missionaries among their people.

When the business of the assembly was completed, the Mohawks promptly urged Jogues and his companions to depart, for if they tarried longer, they were likely to encounter on their homeward journey warriors of the four upper nations, who would certainly kill the two Algonquin deputies and quite possibly the French as well. Jogues was not to be restrained, however, from first making the round of the houses. He instructed the few Christian prisoners still remaining there and heard their confessions, and baptized several dying Mohawks.

Jogues and his party arrived back in Quebec on July 3, where they were warmly congratulated upon their success, Bourdon receiving valuable land grants as a reward. Jogues felt that the peace just concluded would enable him to return to the Mohawks as a missionary. By planting in their hearts the gospel of truth, justice, righteousness, mercy, and love, he would not only lift them out of the morass of depravity, but would also strengthen their resolution to live in friendship with whites and Indians alike. He petitioned his superior to send him back to the Mohawks, this time as an ambassador of God.

"After he had rendered an account of his embassy," reports Father Jerome Lalemant, "he thought of nothing else but of undertaking a second voyage so that he might return thither, and especially before the winter. For he could not endure the thought of being longer absent from his spouse of blood."

Lalemant called Fathers Vimont and Le Jeune, both former superiors, into consultation, and the three Jesuits carefully considered Jogues's plea. They had serious misgivings about permitting him to return; time was needed to prove the peaceful intentions of the Iroquois, whose treachery was notorious. They came to a cautious decision: "It was resolved that, if nothing else occurred, Father Jogues should not go to winter among the Iroquois, but should stay at Montreal or Three Rivers. But that, if some excellent opportunity occurred for going thither, this opportunity must not be rejected."

Jogues prayed with all his heart that Divine Providence would provide the "excellent opportunity." Bidding adieu to the governor and to the Fathers at Quebec, he and Father Gabriel Druillettes stepped into the canoe of two Christian Algonquins and headed for Three Rivers.

In September the opportunity came. The Hurons decided to accept an invitation from the Mohawks to send an embassy to them to arrange further details of the peace. They asked Jogues to lead the expedition.

Now was his chance — and a sudden dread seized him, and cold perspiration broke out on his forehead. In his mind he saw the platform of torture, the sharp teeth crunching his fingers, the knives in his flesh, the fire that seared his bleeding stumps of fingers. There came to him a powerful presentiment of danger. His whole nature recoiled instinctively against the thought of falling into the Indians' hands. But Jogues manfully repressed his involuntary dread and asked simply that he might do God's will. In the chapel of Sainte Marie, he recalled, he had offered his life to God, and he would not now go back upon his promise. He was mindful, too, of the words of his superior in Quebec: "It is credible that if the enterprise succeed for the salvation of this people, it will not produce fruit before they be sprinkled with the blood of martyrs."

To a Jesuit confrere in France, Jogues wrote at this time, "If I be employed in this mission, my heart tells me: *Ibo sed non redibo:* 'I shall go, but I shall not return.' In very truth it will be well with me, it will be a happiness for me, if God will be pleased to complete the sacrifice there where He began it."

He set out from Quebec on September 27, 1646. He was accompanied by Jean de Lalande, a young French *donné* like Goupil and Couture, and by three or four Hurons. Before departing, Jogues had explained to Jean the many dangers to which he would be exposing himself. "It may mean captivity, torture, or death," he said, "or all of them combined." He held out his mutilated hands before the youth and told him of his own presentiment that he would not return. Jean listened quietly but did not quail. He said he wished to accompany Father Isaac and share with him the hardships and the perils of life among the Mohawks, even to torture and death. "That good youth," declares Lalemant, "recognizing the dangers in which he was involving himself in so perilous a journey, protested at his departure that the desire of serving God was leading him into a country where he surely expected to meet death."

Jogues and Lalande met Indians on the journey who told them that the Mohawks, in violation of all their peace pledges, were again on the warpath, murdering their ancient enemies the Hurons and Algonquins as savagely as ever. The Huron guides, alarmed, refused to go further. Jogues and Lalande continued on their way.

Soon they were informed that the enmity of the Mohawks was directed at Jogues as well, for reasons of superstition. On his previous visit, he had left in their care a black chest or box, intending to return. They were suspicious that it contained some secret mischief, and to dissipate their fear, Jogues had opened it and shown them the contents: Mass utensils, clothes, books, beads and ribbons for trading. Having removed their suspicions, as he thought, he locked the trunk and left it in their keeping. Some Huron captives, hoping to gain favor with their Iroquois enemies, played on the suspicious fears of their captors by declaring that the French were sorcerers who by their charms and mummeries had brought a host of evils upon their nation — drought, famine, and pestilence. An epidemic had broken out among the Mohawks, and against it the incantations of their medicine men proved futile. And the caterpillars were eating their corn. Clearly these evils were the work of a demon locked up in the Blackrobe's chest.

A majority of the Mohawks, incited by the Bear clan, howled for vengeance against Jogues and for war with the French. The opposition of the Wolf clan, which still honored the peace treaty, was in vain. The Mohawks whipped themselves into a fury, and two bands of warriors set out on the trail.

Threading their way through the forest between the Mohawk River and Lake George, one of these bands, to their delight and astonishment, came upon Jogues and Lalande. They set upon them, stripped them naked, and beat them furiously. They led them in triumph to Ossernenon, where a wild rabble surrounded them and struck them with fists and clubs. One Indian cut strips of flesh from Isaac's neck and arms, saying, "Let us see if this white flesh is the flesh of an *oki* [demon]."

"I am a man like yourselves," replied Isaac, "'but I do not fear death or torture. I do not know why you would kill me. I come here to confirm the peace and show you the way to Heaven, and you treat me like a dog."

He heard voices from the crowd saying, "You shall die tomorrow. Take courage; we shall not bum you. We shall strike you both with a hatchet and place your heads on the palisade, that your brothers may see you when we take them prisoners."

In the evening of October 18, Jogues, bruised and bleeding, was sitting in the lodge of the elderly squaw with whom he had stayed during his previous captivity. A brave of the Bear clan entered and invited Jogues to a feast. To refuse would have given great offense. He consulted with the squaw, who feared treachery but knew that refusal would deepen the ill feeling. Jogues expressed the hope that by going he might make friends with the young brave and the Bears who had invited him. With some misgiving she agreed that he should go. She sent her grandson, Honatteniate, who was the sworn brother of Ondessonk, along to guard him.

Jogues followed the brave to the lodge of the Bear chief. He had just bent his head to enter, when another Indian, standing concealed within, beside the doorway, struck at him with a hatchet. Instantly Honatteniate shot out his arm to ward off the blow, but the tomahawk glanced off it and sank into the missionary's brain. He fell at the feet of his murderer, who at once finished the work by hacking off his head. The Indians dragged his body through the streets with howls of glee.

Jean de Lalande, left in suspense all through the night, was killed in a similar manner the next morning. The bodies of both men were thrown into the Mohawk River, and their heads were displayed on the points of the palisade which enclosed the village. They remained there through the bleak winter, ghastly reminders to the French, and to their Indian allies, of Mohawk vengeance.

Father Isaac Jogues and Jean de Lalande had gone to join the first of the Jesuit martyrs, René Goupil, in the kingdom of God. With the martyrdom of the priest, there passed from the human scene a man singularly selfless. His only ambition was to spread the Christian Faith among the children of the forest; his only will was to do the will of God as disclosed to him by his superiors and by his conscience. Patient, charitable, heroic, he returned love for hatred, blessings for curses, prayers for abuse. That he remained uncontaminated amid the barbarity and open corruption of life in the Indian villages is evident from his words: "The only sin I can remember during my captivity was that I sometimes looked upon the approach of death with complacency."

"Thus died Isaac Jogues," writes Parkman, "one of the purest examples of Roman Catholic virtue which this Western continent has seen. The priests, his associates, praise his humility, and tell us that it reached the point of self-contempt — a crowning virtue in their eyes; that he regarded himself as nothing, and lived solely to do the will of God as uttered by the lips of his Superiors. They add that, when left to the guidance of his own judgment, his self-distrust made him very slow of decision, but that, when acting under orders, he knew neither hesitation nor fear. With all his gentleness, he had a certain warmth or vivacity of temperament; and we have seen how, during his first captivity, while humbly submitting to every caprice of his tyrants and appearing to rejoice in abasement, a derisive word against his Faith would change the lamb into the lion, and the lips that seemed so tame would speak in sharp, bold tones of menace and reproof."[11]

Father Jerome Lalemant recorded in the *Relation* for 1647 the conviction of the Jesuits at Quebec and of others who knew him well that Isaac Jogues had died a martyr.[12] "It is the thought of several learned men," he writes, "and this idea is more than reasonable, that he is truly a martyr before God who renders witness to

[11] Parkman, *The Jesuits in North America*, 304 ff.

[12] Taking cognizance of this deep conviction, the Fathers of the Plenary Councils of Baltimore and of Quebec petitioned for his formal canonization. At last, after exhaustive investigation, Pope Pius XI, amid solemn ceremonies on June 29, 1930, pronounced the verdict whereby the missionary priest and his two companions were elevated as Saint Isaac, Saint René, and Saint Jean.

Heaven and earth that he values the Faith and the propagation of the gospel more highly than his own life — losing it in the dangers into which, with full consciousness, he cast himself for Jesus Christ, and protesting before His face that he wishes to die in order to make Him known. That death is the death of a Martyr before the Angels. It was with this view that the Father yielded up his soul to Jesus Christ and for Jesus Christ. I say much more than this: not only did he embrace the means for publishing the gospel which have caused his death, but more, one may affirm that he was killed through hatred for the doctrine of Jesus Christ."

≈

Jean de Brébeuf
Gabriel Lalemant

~

Chapter 6

Jean de Brébeuf was one of the most resourceful, stouthearted, and persevering of all the missionaries who worked to evangelize the American Indians. Physically powerful and of towering stature, he was the only one of the eight canonized Jesuit martyrs of North America to exceed fifty years of age. All the others were born and died within the first half of the seventeenth century. He was among the first missionaries to enter Huronia and among the last to leave, and for years he was alone there. He wrote voluminously, revealing even his interior life at the request of his superior. So much did he accomplish and so steadfastly did he labor, that it is scarcely too much to say that in a drama of surpassing characters, he played the leading role.

Brébeuf was born on March 25, 1593, at Condé-sur-Vire, near Lisieux, home of the Little Flower, and not far from Bayeux, famous for its tapestry. He was descended from a noble Normandy family, among whom had been two Crusaders and a Brébeuf who had fought with William the Conqueror in the Battle of Hastings.

Virtually nothing is known of the first twenty-four years of his life. In November 1617, being then twenty-four, he entered the

Society of Jesus at Rouen, and his unfailing obedience to the letter of the law and to its spirit persisted from his noviceship to the end. "I will be ground to powder," he used to say, "rather than break a rule." His sense of humility prompted him to ask to be a lay brother and no more, but his superiors prevailed upon him to work toward the priesthood.

Two years later, on November 8, 1619, he pronounced his first vows and was assigned to teach at the College of Rouen. His health failed him, however, and he could neither teach nor study for the prescribed length of time. At the Jesuit residence at Pontoise he recuperated and covered enough theology to be ordained on February 19, 1622. He celebrated his first Mass on April 4 in the College Church of Rouen, and in the following year he became college treasurer.

When the Récollet missionary Fathers in New France appealed for help in carrying the gospel to the Indians, Brébeuf volunteered. With Fathers Charles Lalemant and Enemond Massé and two lay brothers, he sailed from Dieppe on April 24, 1625.

Emery de Caen, a Huguenot, was commander at Quebec, and when the vessel came into the port at that city, Caen was ready with an unpleasant surprise for the five Jesuits. Declaring they had not the proper credentials, he refused to let them land. Dumbfounded, the Jesuits looked in dismay at one another and at Quebec, a hundred yards away. Then, knowing they had received authorization from the proper officials in France, they protested hotly.

Meanwhile, the superior of the Récollets, Father Joseph Le Caron, had rowed out to the boat. First welcoming the Jesuits, he turned to Caen and demanded that the Jesuits be allowed to stay in Quebec until any necessary legal documents were obtained.

"There is no room for them," said Caen, "either in the fort or in the settlement." The question was neither asked nor answered, whether there would have been room if their credentials had been satisfactory.

"Then I'll make room for them in the Récollet convent," replied Le Caron, "and I'll assume full responsibility for their landing."

Thereupon he took the Jesuits in his boat to the small Récollet residence. Although it was crowded even for the four or five Récollets who were there, Le Caron, with good Franciscan hospitality, gave to the Jesuits the best he had in his poverty.

Le Caron unfolded to the newcomers the story of the avarice and noncooperation of the fur-trading Montmorency Company, and of their failure to develop the colony in return for the fur monopoly granted to them. After Champlain had founded Quebec in 1608 — six years before he invited the Récollets to come to New France and evangelize the Indians — the Huguenot merchants had acquired full control of the trade, which they retained until the British fleet under David Kirk drove out Champlain in 1629.

"Even now," Father Le Caron explained to the Jesuits, "seventeen years after Champlain founded the colony as the beginning of the French Empire in the New World, there are only fifty-one French winter residents in all of New France. The Huguenot bankers and merchants have done nothing toward helping to colonize or to develop the missions; in truth, they have hindered both enterprises at every turn and have caused more trouble than all the savages from Gaspé to Lake Huron."

The Récollet Fathers, however, had little time for futile recriminations, for there was work to do. They helped the Jesuits start a residence of their own, familiarized them with the problems of wilderness travel and Huron conversion, then set out for Three Rivers to meet their fellow Récollet, Father Nicholas Viel, whom we have mentioned earlier. Viel was due back from his labors in Huronia, but when the last canoe of the Indian flotilla had arrived at that trading post, there still was no sign of him. The Récollets inquired anxiously among the Hurons and were met with stony silence.

A rumor soon reached them that the missionary had been drowned in the rapids now known as Sault-au-Récollet, north of Montreal. Soon some of the Indians were seen wearing for ornament various articles of vestment; next, many of the Mass utensils were found hidden in one of the canoes. Bit by bit the tragic story was pieced together. Father Viel had been robbed and murdered by the Hurons with whom he was traveling, and his body thrown into the river. The Récollets later recovered the body and brought it to Quebec for burial.

Although Father Le Caron expressed his belief that the Hurons were the most likely Indians to respond to the missionaries' efforts, this violent incident alarmed Father Charles Lalemant, superior of the Jesuit group, and prompted him to await a more favorable opportunity to send out missionaries to them. Brébeuf had been eager to begin his work, and this delay must have disappointed him, but he accepted the decision with cheerfulness and good grace.

When it was learned, shortly after, that a band of Montagnais Indians near Quebec, where the Jesuits were marking time, would soon set out on a hunting trip into the forest, Brébeuf obtained permission to accompany them. He stepped into one of their canoes on October 20, 1625, and so started his long and turbulent career in the uncharted wilderness of New France.

For work and recreation during the day, there was walking long miles through the forest. For a bed on which to sleep at night, there was a layer of leaves or pine needles on the ground. For food, until game should be caught, there were smoked eels warmed in tepid water. Each morning the squaws added eels to the unwashed kettles, and into the slimy depths reached coppery arms.

Brébeuf soon grew stiff in every limb from the plodding and the trotting. But worse, he was lonely. He could not communicate with his companions, save by gestures. The Indians seemed very different now from the Indians he had observed at the trading settlements. There, they were gay and voluble, outdoing one another with shrill cackles and good-natured grunts. Here, they were stolid and taciturn. There, they had been all helpfulness and understanding. Here, when he pointed at objects and inquired their names, they deliberately confused him and taught him obscenities.

Brébeuf was shocked by their unhygienic habits and their sexual practices. There was no concealment of the body or its functions, and he soon observed that, although braves and squaws formed a kind of family union for begetting and rearing children, promiscuity was general among young and old. If wandering bands of Indians joined his party in hunting or feasting or at the camps along the way, males and females seemed as promiscuous as the dogs. And why he refused their invitations was beyond their understanding.

Deeply mired in animal impulses and webbed in superstition, fantastically committed to manitous and sorcerers, demons and medicine men, volatile, unreliable, unpredictable, prey to lightning-like fears, they would require years of work and the grace of God, reflected Brébeuf, to rise from their degradation. They were mischievous and cunning, arrogant, vengeful, and cruel, and the Jesuit realized the magnitude of the task of reshaping them by education, discipline, and prayer into the spiritual image of Christ. And not for a moment did he flinch at the enterprise into which he had plunged.

As the months of the wintry hunt went by, Brébeuf, while making no apparent progress toward conversion, did commence to master the Montagnais version of the Algonquin language. And

the challenge was no small one, for the lipless, inarticulate voca-
bles were dismaying to cope with at first. The Indians did not seem
to use their mouths at all in speech; rather, they emitted words
from their throats in such manner that the words seemed to origi-
nate in their lungs and stomachs. Only after untiring study was
Brébeuf able to discriminate the meanings of utterances by their
cadence and intonation. His ear was keen, his natural talent for
languages was considerable, and despite the Indians' mischievous
noncooperation, he succeeded that winter in composing a grammar and a dictionary of the language. More important still, by slow
degree he had softened the hearts of the Indians and won their respect and admiration.

After five months in the piercing cold and the primitive life of
the forest, the party returned to the St. Lawrence. On March 27,
1626, two days after his thirty-third birthday, Brébeuf was joyously
welcomed at the gate of the Récollet garden. In his absence, the
Jesuit residence had been nearly completed. Father Lalemant had
also accompanied a band of Montagnais into the forest, but after a
week they returned for lack of game.

Near the end of June, five vessels arrived at Tadoussac, one hundred twenty-five miles down river from Quebec, with reinforcements of three Jesuits: Father Philibert Noyrot, Father Anne de
Noüe, and Brother Jean Gaufestre. They arrived at Quebec on
July 14. At this time, to add to the cheerful excitement, Champlain assumed full control of Quebec as lieutenant governor. Emery de Caen was permitted to superintend the fur trading during
the summer but was forbidden to stay in Quebec. This, of course,
would mean full support for the missionaries, who under Caen had
had none.

Father Lalemant believed that conditions were favorable for
sending missionaries into Huronia. Preparations were made for

the thousand-mile journey, which would be undertaken by the two Jesuits Brébeuf and Noüe and the Récollet Father de la Roche. They would accompany the Huron party that had been trading at Quebec. Places were found in the canoes for Roche and Noüe, but the Indians demurred at taking Brébeuf because of his great size; finally, a brave was persuaded by generous gifts to take him.

The flotilla set out from Quebec on July 25, 1625. The route would take them along the Ottawa and Nipissing rivers, down the French River to Georgian Bay, and out from the Bay into Lake Huron. Jean remained crouched in the canoe for hours, scarcely daring to move for fear of irritating the fretful Indians. Save for the lapping of the water against the sides of the canoe, and the grunts of the Indians, Brébeuf was in a silent world of river and forest. His back ached and his legs grew cramped from the discomfort of his motionless position, and relief did not come until the sun was setting and the Redskins pulled to shore. After a supper of watery cornmeal, the natives stretched out around the campfire and, oblivious of the swarming mosquitoes, were soon fast asleep.

Brébeuf writes vividly of the trails and waters he followed during this trip:

> Of two ordinary difficulties, the chief is that of the rapids and gorges. . . . All the rivers of this country are full of them, and notably the St. Lawrence after that of the Prairies is passed. For from there onward it is no longer a smooth bed, but is broken up in several places, rolling and leaping in a frightful way, like an impetuous torrent; and even in some places, it falls down suddenly from an enormous height. Now, when these rapids or torrents are reached, it is necessary to land, and carry on the shoulder, through woods or over high and troublesome rocks, all the baggage and the

canoes themselves. This is not done without much work, for there are portages of one, two, and three leagues, and for each several trips must be made, no matter how few packages one has.

In some places, where the current is not less strong than in these rapids, although easier at first, the savages get into the water, and haul and guide by hand their canoes with extreme difficulty and danger; for they sometimes get in up to the neck and are compelled to let go their hold, saving themselves as best they can from the rapidity of the water, which snatches their canoe from them and bears it off. . . . I kept count of the number of portages, and found that we carried our canoes thirty-five times, and dragged them at least fifty.

The second ordinary difficulty that Brébeuf mentions is that of the food, which normally consists of no more than Indian corn mashed between two stones. "Add to these difficulties," he points out, "that one must sleep on the bare earth, or on a hard rock, for lack of space ten or twelve feet square on which to place a wretched hut; that one must endure continually the stench of tired-out savages, and must walk in water, in mud, in the obscurity and entanglement of the forest, where the stings of an infinite number of mosquitoes and gnats are a serious annoyance. . . . We all had to begin by these experiences to bear the cross that our Lord presents to us for His honor, and for the salvation of these poor barbarians. In truth, I was sometimes so weary that the body could do no more, but at the same time my soul experienced very deep peace, considering that I was suffering for God."

The Hurons, who had been so reluctant to take on the heroically built Brébeuf, found him an admirable traveler. He had paddled his share, he was not sick, he had been invariably pleasant, and apparently he had not rocked the boat. Seeing him pick up a heavy pack and carry it with back unbent over a long portage, the Hurons named him "Echon," meaning "The man-who-carries-the-load."

At last the long journey against buffeting currents and over long portages was ended, and the canoes were beached on the shores of Penetanguishene Bay, off the larger Georgian Bay. The missionaries had traveled in widely separated groups of the flotilla, and now Brébeuf was escorted by the Indians a short distance inland to the Huron village of Toanché.[13] When he looked at the copper-skinned natives who thronged to see him, he felt with uprising joy that he had at last found his clients; they would be his children, and he their father, and he would stay with them to the end.

Brébeuf learned that Father de la Roche had arrived at another village, and shortly afterward he was rejoined by Father de Noüe, who had not made an altogether good impression during the trip. Fresh from France, and not having had the benefit of an apprenticeship such as Brébeuf had undergone the winter before, he had suffered from hunger and retchings and the terrifying loneliness of the wilds. His unadaptability had occasioned angry whacks from the Indians, and from these he suffered also. To be in the protective company of Father Jean de Brébeuf was a relief.

Toanché was a cluster of about fifteen longhouses, rectangular and permanent. They ranged in length from twenty to eighty feet, and in each, depending upon its length, dwelt six to twenty families. They were afflicted with the shortcomings and annoyances universally found among Indian habitations. The smoke inflamed

[13]Seven miles northwest of the site of the present-day Martyr's Shrine near Midland, Ontario, which is about ninety miles north of Toronto.

the eyes, there was no privacy, the stench of decaying food and urine, of grease and human bodies, floated through the thick atmosphere. Lice and fleas infested the bunks and clothing; mice and rats scurried across the floor. It was all very trying, particularly so to Nouë, a man of more than usually delicate sensibilities who had had no experience in the primitive life.

Brébeuf observed that the Hurons were taller than the Montagnais Indians and the French, and they were lithe and muscular. Their hair was abundant, straight as wires, and jet black, while they were hairless on chin and body. In the cabins, and during warm weather, the men went naked, except for a breech cloth or a dangling pad of leather. The older women, Brébeuf recorded, wore a skin or cloth hanging loosely from shoulder to knee; the young women wore only a short skirt about their hips. Children of both sexes went perfectly naked.

With all their crudities, Brébeuf found the Hurons friendly and hospitable. "They never close their door to a stranger," he writes, "and having once received him in their houses, they share with him the best of what they have and never send him away. When he leaves of his own accord, he acquits his debt with a simple thank you." Under this system, the two Blackrobes were at liberty to live in any cabin they chose, eat from any pot, and remain with any family as long as they wished.

Soon after they had settled, Brébeuf and Nouë visited the Récollet Father de la Roche at the village where he was staying, Quieunonascaran. This was the capital village of the Bear nation, and it was fortified by a triple row of palisades, the posts being twenty feet high and closely planted. Within the crowded enclosure were about fifty longhouses, containing some five hundred families. It was one of the largest Huron villages, and its leaders were among the most powerful of all the Huron peoples.

The Jesuits found Roche dwelling in a lodge built ten years before for Father Le Caron and used since then by the Récollets and the French fur traders. The lodge was divided into three rooms, and Roche invited the Jesuits to stay on with him there. Brébeuf, desirous of learning the language and habits of the Hurons, declined the tempting offer.

The three missionaries went to pay their respects to the chiefs and elders of the Bear nation assembled in Quieunonascaran. They were welcomed cordially by the chiefs, who pledged them peace and friendship while the braves applauded with vigorous belly laughs.

Back at Toanché, Brébeuf applied himself to the multiple tasks of mastering the Huron tongue, examining their customs, and learning their beliefs. Before he could admit them to Baptism, he would have to root out their superstitions and wean them from their inveterate vices. He realized the dimensions of the problem, for the practices of the Hurons were similar to those he had noted among the Montagnais. Even as the Montagnais had done, the Hurons satisfied their sexual instincts with little decency or control, and expected the missionaries to do likewise. The Jesuits were continually embarrassed by being pursued by the Indian women, who begged them to marry them or make some sort of family alliance. The women and girls importuned them more insistently even than did the men, who actively petitioned them on behalf of the females. What made it more difficult for the missionaries to resist plausibly the advances of the women and explain to the men that such conduct was contrary to the Christian code, was the example of some of the French agents who lived among the Hurons and became fully as degraded as Indians in their practices.

Fortified by grace, however, the missionaries were immune. Brébeuf's chastity, wrote his confessor, "was proof; and in that matter his eyes were so faithful to his heart that they had no sight for the objects which might have soiled purity. His body was not rebellious to the spirit; and in the midst of impurity itself — which reigns, it seems, in this country — he lived in an innocence as great as if he had sojourned in the midst of a desert inaccessible to that sin. A woman presented herself one day to him, in a place somewhat isolated, uttering to him unseemly language, and breathing a fire which could come only from a firebrand of Hell. The Father, seeing himself thus attacked, made upon himself the Sign of the Cross, without answering any word; and this specter, disguised beneath a woman's dress, disappeared at the same moment."

On October 26 Father de la Roche set out with two French agents to visit the Petuns toward the west, proposing to winter among the Neutrals in the south. In so doing, the Récollet was following the advice of Father Le Caron in opening new mission fields, and of Champlain in suggesting alliances and attracting these nations to the French trade. Late in the winter, rumors reached Toanché that Roche was being badly treated by the Neutrals. Brébeuf persuaded a French agent to make the six-day journey and bring the missionary back if he still survived.

Roche and the agent returned toward the end of March. For three months, he reported, he had been hospitably entertained by the Neutrals, but then Huron mischief-makers came on the scene. "They told the Neutrals that I was a powerful magician, that I tainted the air in the Huron country, that I had already poisoned many Huron people, that I was going to be killed soon to prevent me from setting fire to the village and burning all the children to death."

In spite of the difficulties brought down upon him, Roche was convinced that the Neutrals could be converted more easily than the Hurons, and could be persuaded to form alliances with the French for peace and trade.

The Récollet found no Huron converts upon his return, but he observed a marked reformation effected by the Blackrobes upon the French agents. "What consoled me," he wrote, "on my return from the Neutrals was to see that our fellow countrymen had made their peace with our Lord, for they confessed and received Communion at Easter. They have put away their women, and since then have been more restrained."

The old Récollet cabin at Quieunonascaran, through age, continual use, and general decrepitude, had become uninhabitable, and the three missionaries had a new cabin built for themselves and the French agents near Toanché. Instead of the totems that adorned the cabins of the Hurons, they hung a large wooden cross above the door and painted it red. Here the priests could pray without being suspected of witchery; here they would be spared the vermin, the stenches, the promiscuous sexuality, the orgies of the sorcerers — with which by now they were all too familiar. In this cabin, perhaps, a chapel might one day be fitted out where Mass would be celebrated.

Meanwhile, Father Anne de Noüe was not making much progress with the difficult Huron language, and in spite of his brave intentions, the primitive ways of the Indians were too much for his fine sensibilities. Accordingly, Brébeuf thought it advisable for him to return to Quebec, where he could be of genuine service. In June this saintly man, who had borne the crudities of the Indians and the hardships of life without complaint, joined a large flotilla of Hurons and French agents leaving for the trade at Cap de la Victoire.

When the French agents returned in September, they brought dismal news from Quebec. Father Noyrot had left Honfleur, France, with provisions for the Jesuits and their workmen, but the vessel was thought to have lost its way. Expecting a shortage of food during the coming winter, Father Charles Lalemant was obliged to send the Jesuit workmen back to France. For another reason, he himself followed them to the mother country: he had been deputed by Champlain and the Récollets to represent them in France in the continuing struggle against Caen and the Montmorency Company, who were showing no inclination to support the interests of New France.

Saddest of all to Brébeuf in the immediate picture was the fact that no Jesuit had come with the flotilla to help him in the lonely struggle to evangelize Huronia.

Now, many of the Huron braves, streaked with black and crimson paint, flourishing tomahawks, and tittering bloodcurdling battle cries, were whirling off on the warpath against their traditional enemies, the Iroquois. Not long after, some commenced to return, wailing over the death of their comrades. Others led back their captives and proudly displayed the scalps that dangled from their belts. Of this Brébeuf noted:

> When they capture some of their enemies, they treat them
> with all the cruelty they can devise. Five or six days will
> sometimes pass in assuaging their fury and in burning them
> at slow fires. Not satisfied with roasting their skin, they slash
> the legs, the thighs, the arms, and the fleshiest parts, and
> thrust glowing brands or red-hot hatchets against them. . . .
> After having finally killed the victims, they tear out their
> hearts if they were brave men, roast them on the embers,
> and distribute pieces of them to the young people. They con-
> sider that this will make them brave. Others make incisions
> in the upper part of the throats of their own young men, and
> cause some of the dead man's blood to run into it; they say
> that since the blood of the enemy has been mingled with

theirs, they will never be surprised by him and will be enabled to know of his approach, however secret it may be. . . .

The victims are put into the caldron piece by piece; although at other feasts, the head, whether of a dog, bear, deer, or big fish, is the portion of the chief, in this case the head is given to the lowest person. Some taste this dish and the rest of the body only with much horror. But there are some who eat it with pleasure. I have observed savages speaking with gusto of the flesh of an Iroquois, and praising its goodness in the same terms they use for the flesh of a deer or moose. . . . This is being cruel; but we hope, with the help of Heaven, that the knowledge of the true God will entirely banish such barbarity from this country.

As Brébeuf studied their beliefs, he gradually came to perceive the enormous importance they attached to their dreams. These ruled and tyrannized their whole life. If even a chief of the tribe argues one way, a dream will prevail if it argues differently. "A dream," writes Brébeuf, "prescribes the feasts, the dances, the songs, the games; in a word, the dream does everything here, and in truth, is to be regarded as the chief god of the Hurons."

High confidence was likewise placed in their charms, for which their word was *oki,* meaning also "demon." A fish bone, a queerly shaped pebble, a beaver's tooth, or the ashes of a bird would be consulted as to what course they should pursue: in such objects resided demons, who had power to help or to hinder and who must under all circumstances be obeyed.

Brébeuf noticed also the power of the sorcerers, who swayed the lives of the natives at every turn. They claimed power to control the weather, to find lost objects, and to predict future events. To cure the sick, they prescribed remedies that had not the slightest relation to the illness. They believed that all diseases were caused by little demons that crept into the body of the victim, and these they would try to frighten away. For guidance in the appropriate ritual to accomplish this, they turned to dreams, *okis*, and incantations. In certain cases, the sorcerers would prescribe elaborate ceremonials, such as the fire dance, the nude dance, the festival of the madmen, or such ritual feasts as the "eat-all" or the "vomit" feasts. The sorcerers were obeyed down to the smallest detail, and so were a constant menace to the health and sanity of the natives.

The missionaries would try to explain to the people the lack of causal relation between sicknesses and their prescribed cures, and so were viewed with suspicion, jealousy, and hatred by the sorcerers. Some of the missionaries thought that the Hurons recognized no God, but worshiped only a demon, or *oki*; others thought, more specifically, that they had a good demon and a bad demon. Brébeuf, who lived closest to them, and over the longest period of any of the Jesuits, was of the opinion that the Hurons had a faint, hazy notion of God, but that this notion was not strong or clear enough to prompt them to serve or to honor Him. They did believe in survival of the soul after death, but the soul was regarded as a material object.

The Hurons appeared not to have a concept of reward or punishment after death, but during the span of earthly life, they did fear the wrath of the Great Oki, the power that regulated the seasons, the elements, and other forces. To propitiate this power and obtain its aid, they would throw tobacco into the flames, sacrifice living animals, and offer the flesh of victims of violent death. These practices would seem to confirm Brébeuf's view that the Hurons had some perverted notion of God and were a degenerate people clinging to a remnant of a revelation their ancestors had possessed.

"This people," he writes, "is not so stupefied that it does not seek and acknowledge something more lofty than the senses. Since their licentious life and their lewdness prevent them from finding God, it is very easy for the devil to insinuate himself and to offer them his services in the urgent need in which he sees them. . . . May He who has saved us by the blood of the Immaculate Lamb consent to remedy these [superstitions] as soon as possible, accepting for this purpose, if need be, our souls and our lives, which we most freely offer to Him for the salvation of these peoples and the remission of our sins."

Gradually mastering the Huron language, Brébeuf was puzzled in his quest for some means to express spiritual and abstract concepts so that the Hurons could grasp them. Their vocabulary, as he also had discovered in the case of the Montagnais, was limited to concrete, sensuous objects; they had no word for a supreme being, God. They could comprehend the idea only through some such circumlocution as "He-who-made-all" or "He-who-knows-all." Through similar manipulation of words, Brébeuf succeeded in translating into Huron the catechism of Ledesma, a basic pamphlet of four short chapters. This was to serve as a handbook for future missionaries and spare them the grubbing labor he had expended.

In the spring, Father de la Roche decided to go to Quebec. He and Brébeuf, living alone in their cabin, badly needed artifacts from the French with which to barter for their food. Also their garments were tattered, and needed replacing. Furthermore, the Récollet was feeling the strain of primitive living, and would benefit from rest and a change. Even more important, he wished to report to his superior, Father Le Caron, and to Champlain and the French fur-trade directors the advantages, which they had long suspected, of cultivating the Neutrals as well as the Hurons, and independently of these.

Near the end of June, Roche joined a large convoy of Huron canoes about to start their journey down the Ottawa River to Cap de la Victoire. With them went the French agents and their annual load of peltries. Roche bade an affectionate farewell to his Jesuit confrere, stepped into a waiting canoe, and was on his way. Brébeuf was alone in the Indians' wilderness.

Brébeuf had been two years at Toanché. For all his unwearying zeal and unending efforts, he had not baptized a single adult Huron. He had received no reinforcements to carry on the unequal struggle; indeed, his two fellow laborers had gone back to Quebec.

What could one priest do in this very heart of paganism? Little by himself, he thought, much with God. Brébeuf had accomplished wonders with the opaque Huron language, and with this advantage he would press on even more vigorously in his third year to explain to the natives the saving truths of Christianity.

In the summer of 1628, a terrible drought fell upon all Huronia. Months passed and not a drop of rain fell on the parched fields. The country was dry as tinder, and fires sprang up everywhere. The corn was drying out; famine the following winter loomed. The squaws were growing hysterical at the prospect. The thumping of the tortoise drum echoed drearily day and night as the sorcerers persevered in their dances and in their incantations to stir the Thunder Bird into action, but it was in vain.

Finally one of the leading sorcerers, Tehorenhaegnon, announced to the villagers that his demon had revealed the cause of his own failure to bring rain: the Thunder Bird would not bring the clouds because it feared the red cross on the Blackrobe's house.

One of the chiefs summoned Brébeuf and said to him, "You do not wish to be the cause of our deaths. We believe that you should take down that red cross and hide it in your cabin or in the lake, so that the clouds may not see it. Then, when the rain comes and the harvest is gathered, you may put it up again."

"My uncle," replied Echon, "I shall never take down or hide the cross on which He-who-brings-blessings died. I cannot prevent you from removing it, but be on your guard against the Master-of-all when He is angry. What Tehorenhaegnon tells you is nonsense, as you can see for yourselves; for since that cross has been there, you have often had an abundance of rain."

"It is not so much the cross," rejoined the chief. "It is mostly the color."

Brébeuf was aware of the Huron belief that thunder is the result of a celestial turkey flapping its wings, and that no turkey takes kindly to red; he thought therefore he might well humor them, so he painted the cross white.

The drought continued in its burning fury, and the wrath of the crazed Hurons fell upon the sorcerer. Then Brébeuf made a proposal.

"Come here tomorrow," he said, "and let us honor the cross after the Christian fashion, and we shall see if we can get rain."

Echon painted the cross red again and hung on it a small crucifix. When the Hurons came the next morning, he recited some prayers. Then he and the Hurons in turn kissed the crucifix.

"On that same day," relates Brébeuf, "God gave them rain, and in the end a plentiful harvest as well as a profound admiration for the Divine Power."

In consequence, Brébeuf became in their eyes a great sorcerer. This was a title of distinction, but it was fraught with danger: anyone could kill a sorcerer when he failed to produce results. But the halo was his for the rest of his life among the Hurons, and it was not a comfortable one; he walked always under threat of death.

The Huron traders returned that fall in a state of unholy wrath. The French had not come to meet them at Cap de la Victoire, and the Indians were obliged to return with their load of furs instead of the French goods they so badly needed. From the agents, Brébeuf learned that Quebec had been hungering all through the previous winter and spring, for Caen had not sent food or articles enough for the Huron trade. More, the French fleet had not come that summer, and it was rumored that English ships were anchored at Tadoussac to intercept them if they appeared.

This was shocking news. It meant that Brébeuf would be without the food, clothing, beads, and French artifacts he needed for the coming year. Even more disheartening was the news that no French priest would be with him.

Alone among the fickle Indians, without the consolation of Confession or the support and companionship of priestly confreres, and thus deprived of all human aid in his superhuman enterprise, Jean de Brébeuf threw himself upon the aid and mercy of God. More than ever he must find in God the strength, the will, and the courage to live the interior life so perfectly that he could transcend the crudeness of his pagan environment.

He attests that God did not fail him: "As for the dangers of the soul, to speak frankly, there is none for him who brings the fear and love of God to the Huron country. On the contrary, I find unparalleled advantages for acquiring perfection." It was an echo of St. Paul: "Who is there who can hurt you if you be zealous of good?"

Over the lonely winter months, Brébeuf spoke more frequently to the Hurons about God, Jesus Christ, and His gospel of love and mercy. He spoke to them also by his unselfish, holy, Christlike life; he visited the sick in their cabins and strove to be their servant in all things. He was still not prepared to make converts, except in the case of Hurons in danger of death; only in this circumstance, since he wanted no backsliders or apostates, did he deem it prudent to baptize them after they had been instructed in the fundamentals of the Christian Faith.

A French agent came to Brébeuf's cabin late the following May. He had been sent by Champlain, and he carried a letter from Father Enemond Massé. The agent reported to Brébeuf that the French were starving at Quebec. The summer before, the English had threatened Quebec and had captured the French fleet. There was every danger that the English or the French Huguenots would again blockade the St. Lawrence and possibly attack Quebec. Brébeuf and the French traders among the Hurons were to come to Quebec, bringing as much corn as they could obtain from the natives. Massé's letter reiterated Champlain's order to hasten back.

Brébeuf was stunned. His dreams of launching a great crusade among the Hurons were shattered. He had conquered their language and their hearts. He knew their minds, their beliefs, their very impulses. He was in a position to influence them strongly toward the Christian Faith. Now this would all have to wait. In God's good time he would return; he had laid a firm groundwork, and one day he would erect here the edifice of Christianity.

The Hurons were genuinely heartbroken. He had won his way into their hearts and was high in their esteem. "We have asked you," said one old man, "to teach us more. What shall we do when you go away?"

One of Brébeuf's last acts before departing was to baptize a baby boy at the request of a brave who had absorbed the missionary's teaching and wanted his boy to be raised a Christian.

In mid-June the twelve canoes of Brébeuf's party and the eight canoes of the French agents and their Huron companions, loaded with as much corn as was possible to bring, struck out from the cove below Toanché. It was spring, and the Ottawa River would be swollen with the thaws. The cascades would be frothing cata-racts, and the stiff current would repeatedly threaten to pull their canoes into the rapids. Danger would certainly dog them all the way.

Manfully, the French and Hurons paddled and portaged the hundreds of miles of tortuous waterways and forest trails, and on the evening of July 17, after a month of feverish struggle, the party came abreast of Quebec's bristling rock and pushed their canoes to the shore. The French inhabitants greeted them with joyous shouts and quickly unloaded the bark casks of precious corn. Champlain hurried from the fort to welcome them, eyeing with some concern the supply of corn, which was, in relation to the mouths it would have to feed and the time it would have to last, somewhat meager.

From Notre Dame des Anges hurried Father Massé, Anne de Noüe, and the three Jesuit brothers. Staring at Jean de Brébeuf as if they could scarcely believe their eyes, they kept murmuring, "Thank God! Thank God! You have come in time!"

~

Chapter 7

Things had been going from bad to worse for the French at Quebec. The English, determined to extend their sway over the whole of the New World, had their navy patrolling the sea lanes to the colony. Not a single French vessel was able to slip through the blockade, and the colonists' food supply was dwindling almost to the vanishing point.

On July 10, 1628, the English fleet under David Kirk appeared before Quebec and demanded immediate surrender. Although the fort had only fifty pounds of gunpowder and a daily food ration of less than two ounces a person, Champlain put on a strong show of force and bluffed the English into withdrawing.

The winter brought increasing misery. Scurvy had broken out, and fresh mounds were dotting the little cemetery. By spring most of the colonists had abandoned the settlement and were scouring the woods and streams for game and fish; some were living on acorns and roots.

That June, Father Philibert Noyrot, whose expedition the previous year had been unsuccessful, organized another voyage to bring desperately needed food and supplies to the New World.

This time his ship was wrecked off Cape Canso, Nova Scotia, and he and Brother Malot lost their lives.

David Kirk sailed his fleet before Quebec again on July 19. Champlain, knowing that further resistance would be futile, capitulated. On the next day, the cross of St. George replaced the fleur-de-lis above the fort.

By the terms of surrender, Récollets and Jesuits were to be expelled and were forbidden to take anything with them except their clothes and books. It was a bitter experience for the missionaries — most of all, perhaps, for Father Enemond Massé, who was undergoing the frustration of exile for the second time: he had been driven out of Acadia by the English in 1613.

Heavy in heart, Jean de Brébeuf lovingly bound in leather his Montagnais dictionary, his Huron phrase book, dictionary, and grammar, and his Huron translation of Ledesma's catechism. Blood and tears of anguish had gone into the making of these, and it is little wonder that even the resilient spirits of the strapping Brébeuf should be depressed. Tears came into his eyes as he stood on the deck of a French vessel with Massé, Roche, Nouë, and the others, and watched the Rock of Quebec disappear behind Point Levis, and the Island of Orléans slip past. They were leaving behind them the country of the Indians, to whose salvation they had dedicated their lives, their labors, and their prayers. Their dream was fading, and they could only commend their future into the hands of God.

Their vessel put in at Tadoussac on the St. Lawrence. They encountered the Huguenot Emery de Caen there, and they were startled to learn from him that France and England had concluded peace in April, three months before. What would this mean for Quebec and the missions? It meant, first of all, that David Kirk's seizure of Quebec was not legal; that it was, in effect, an act of piracy.

But, as always, nine-tenths of the law of nations was possession, and there were no means at hand to force Kirk and the new occupants of Quebec to relinquish what they had improperly taken and to depart quietly. Kirk held out, solid and entrenched, upon the Rock.

The French weighed anchor and continued on to their mother country. The moment he arrived, Champlain commenced to prod the government into action. He had to overcome mountains of lethargy on the part of French officialdom if his country were not to lose by default what Madame de Pompadour was later to call "a few acres of snow." Three long years of unflagging effort were rewarded: Canada was restored to France on March 25, 1632, by the Treaty of Saint-Germain-en-Laye. Champlain, the founder of New France, now became its savior. His lieutenant, Bouchard, was despatched at once to take possession of Quebec, and with Bouchard went the Jesuits Father Anne de Nouë, Brother Buret, and Father Le Jeune, who was to be the superior of the reestablished missions.

Meanwhile, during this exile from the New World, Jean de Brébeuf continued to be active. Reassigned to the Jesuit College at Rouen, he made his final year of probation there. Known also as the tertianship, this period was given over to the crowning preparation of the Jesuit for his life's work. It was a year of prayer, meditation, study, and spiritual exercises. Brébeuf pronounced his final vows as a Jesuit on January 30, 1630.

He was then appointed treasurer of the small Jesuit college in Eu. Not only did he perform this new duty with fidelity, but in the spirit of his youthful assertion that he would "be ground to powder before breaking a rule," he did so with unabated zeal, almost as if his heart were not still with the Hurons. Daily he prayed that he might be sent back to them. In his journal he wrote, "I have felt an ardent desire to suffer something for Jesus Christ. I fear I shall be refused, because our Lord has thus far treated me with kindness, whereas I have grievously offended His Divine Majesty. I shall be more confident of salvation when God will give me a chance to suffer."

And he made this vow: "Lord Jesus, my Redeemer! You have redeemed me by Your Blood and Your most precious death. That is why I promise to serve You all my life in the Society of Jesus and never to serve any other. I sign this promise in my blood, ready to sacrifice it all for You as willingly as this drop." He was offering his life to God.

Brébeuf's prayers were answered. When Champlain, now accredited as "Captain of the King's Navy and Lieutenant of His Lordship the Cardinal [Richelieu] throughout the whole length of the St. Lawrence," sailed from Dieppe on March 23, 1633, at his side stood Jean de Brébeuf.

The little fleet entered the St. Lawrence early in May, but floating ice prevented them from reaching Quebec until several weeks later. The cannon on the fort thundered a hearty welcome and signaled the return of the exiled Brébeuf after nearly five years. He was so jubilant that when he touched shore, he kissed the ground and knelt in prayer. "God knows," wrote Le Jeune, "that we received and embraced him with glad hearts."

The English, during their occupation, had undone much of what the French had accomplished. The Jesuits' residence had been heavily damaged and would have to be repaired, but this was nothing to compare with the demoralizing influence the English had had upon the Indians. They had sold them firewater, which caused the men and women to get drunk and fight and kill one another, and they had to some extent managed by this and other means to disaffect the natives toward the French. There was much to do.

On July 28 a swarm of Hurons, numbering six or seven hundred, came paddling to Quebec for their annual trading session. There were many who remembered Brébeuf, their beloved Echon, and they greeted him with genuine affection. In the case of Champlain, they were a little uncertain. A group of Hurons had killed a French agent, Étienne Brulé, and they were apprehensive that the governor might work revenge.

Champlain, however, was in no mood to alienate the Hurons, whose trade and friendship were an important factor to be considered. The cautious respect that the Hurons exhibited toward Champlain was reciprocated by a full display of goodwill on his part. He explained to them that he did not plan to avenge the death of Brulé, who had in various ways proved himself a traitor to the French and was well gotten rid of. Champlain made it clear that he was eager to resume trading with the Hurons, and desired further that they should agree upon mutual friendship and protection.

The relieved Indians wasted no time exchanging furs and tobacco for hatchets, knives, kettles, cloth, beads, iron arrowheads, coats, shirts, and other articles, and during their stay, they were feasted by the French. They expressed their renewed devotion to the French in many ways, and solid harmony reigned.

Champlain next introduced to the assembled natives the three newly arrived missionaries, Jean de Brébeuf, Antoine Daniel, and Ambroise Davost. "These are our fathers," he said. "We love them more than we love ourselves. The whole French nation honors them. They do not go among you for furs. They have left their friends and their country to show you the way to Heaven. If you love the French, as you say you love them, then love and honor these our fathers."

Deeply impressed, the Indians readily agreed to take the Blackrobes back with them to Huronia. Thereupon the governor led the chiefs into the chapel, and the priests explained the statues and pictures to them. The Hurons were shown three images of the Virgin and were told who she was. Puzzled, "How could Christ have three mothers?" they asked.

On the eve of departure, Brébeuf, Daniel, and Davost took their baggage to the storehouse, and there they passed the night. The Hurons were encamped about them. At eleven that night, the priests were awakened by a loud voice in the Indian camp. Looking out, they saw an Indian chief walking among the natives, haranguing them in angry tones. This was Le Borgne — One Eye — who was chief of the Algonquin tribe *La Nation de l'Isle,* which occupied the Island of the Allumettes in the Ottawa River. Members of this tribe had accompanied the Hurons on the present trading expedition.

Brébeuf listened carefully to what Le Borgne was saying. "We have begged the French captain," the priest heard, "to spare the life of the Algonquin of *La Petite Nation* whom he keeps in prison, but he will not listen to us. The prisoner will die. Then his people will revenge him. They will try to kill the three Blackrobes whom you are about to carry to your country. If you do not defend them, the French will be angry and charge you with their death. But if you do defend them, the Algonquins will make war on you, and the river will be closed. If the French captain will not let the prisoner go, then leave the three Blackrobes where they are; for, if you take them with you, they will bring you to trouble."

Greatly disturbed, the priests hurried to the fort, aroused Champlain, and told him what they had heard. He sent his interpreter to tell the Hurons that he wished to speak with them before their departure. The chiefs assembled and the governor addressed them. He tried persuasion, then promises, and finally threats, but in vain. Le Borgne had successfully played upon the fears of the Hurons, convincing them that if the Algonquin prisoner of the French were not released, the Blackrobes would surely be murdered, and war would follow.

Le Borgne had two objectives. One was to drive a wedge between the Hurons and the French, so that his own tribe might benefit more fully from relations with the colonists; the other was to gain credit and influence with the Algonquin nation to which the prisoner belonged, by securing his release. Meanwhile, he would not prejudice his own friendship with the Hurons.

Champlain refused to release the prisoner, who had been apprehended for murdering a Frenchman in cold blood. He felt that it would place the French in a position of weakness to condone the murder in the first place, and to yield to threats from the Algonquin chief in the second. The upshot was that the Hurons declined to take the Jesuits with them, even though the priests offered to assume all the risks and not to involve their native friends.

It was a keen disappointment to them, for they had been impatient to resume their missionary endeavors among the Hurons. The Indians paddled away, and the priests had no choice but to make other plans. Among the tribes that made their home in the neighborhood of Quebec, paganism and degraded practices were universal. Brébeuf decided to work toward evangelizing these people while his associates, in addition to helping him, would study the Huron language and so prepare for future labors in Huronia. The Jesuits followed this schedule for a year, and made several remarkable conversions among the natives. Brébeuf fortified his old conviction that, properly instructed and seduced from their superstitious beliefs and immoral practices, the American Indians would make earnest and devout Christians.

During this time, grievous calamities had befallen the Hurons. A pestilence had broken out among them, and its ravages had taken many lives. Then, the following summer, five hundred of them, laden with furs, were paddling down the St. Lawrence to trade with the French, when they were ambushed by the Iroquois. In the fight that followed, two hundred Hurons were slain and another hundred taken captive. The battered remnants, instead of continuing on to Quebec, as planned, stopped off at Three Rivers to seek the protection of the French.

When they had patched their wounds and had done what trading was left them to do, the French renewed their earnest request of the year before that they take with them the three missionaries, Brébeuf, Daniel, and Davost, on their return trip to Huronia, along with a few French workmen who would assist the priests. The Indians were plainly reluctant to do so; but when they were loaded with presents, their adamant refusal finally gave way to fretful compliance. In surly mood they took the Frenchmen into their canoes and set out.

The long journey, beset with rapids and cascades, long overland hauls, and unabating danger from the Iroquois, was made all the more trying for the missionaries by the bad tempers of the Hurons, many of whom were sick with fever. Davost's Indian robbed him of part of his baggage, threw most of his books and writing paper into the river, then abandoned him with the Algonquins on the Island of the Allumettes. Daniel also was abandoned, but he managed to find another party of Hurons who took him into their canoe.

Brébeuf, describing some of the severe hardships of the journey, wrote, "Whoever comes here must be prepared for all this, and something more, even death itself, whose image is every moment before our eyes. Not knowing how to swim, I had a very narrow escape. As we were leaving the Bissiriniens, while shooting a rapid we would have gone over a high falls, had not my savages promptly and skillfully leaped into the water to turn aside the ca-noe which the current was sweeping."

On August 5, 1634, thirty days after leaving Three Rivers, Brébeuf neared the north shore of Penetanguishene Bay. The ill-tempered natives unceremoniously landed him there, some dis-tance from the spot where he had first disembarked in Huronia eight years before. They threw his baggage on the shore after him and prepared to make off.

Seeing no sign of human habitation in any direction, Brébeuf asked, "Are you going to leave me here? Will you not lead me to the nearest village? Will you not at least stay to watch these goods while I go to hunt for someone?"

They made no answer.

"Do you forget all I did for you?" he asked. "How I nursed you on the way up when you were sick, and cared for you when you were injured? Will you not at least keep your promise?"

They glared at him in sullen silence and paddled away, and there he was left alone in the wilderness. For their surly ill-treatment, the ever-charitable Brébeuf was prepared to excuse them, "for we know very well," he says, "how sickness alters the disposition and the inclinations of even the most sociable."

When the Hurons had left him, he knelt in prayer to thank God, who in His Providence had seen him safely through all his perils.

"I prostrated myself upon my knees," he wrote to Le Jeune, "to thank God, our Lady, and Saint Joseph for the favors and mercies I had received during the journey. I saluted the guardian angel of the country. I offered myself, with all my feeble labors, to our Lord, for the salvation of these poor peoples. Since our Lord had pre-served me and guided me with so much goodness, I took hope that He would not abandon me here."

Rising, Brébeuf hid his baggage in the woods, including the utensils for Mass, more precious than all the rest. It was not long before he got his bearings and found the trail to Toanché.

It was in ashes. Some charred poles remained of the chapel where he had made his effort to establish a beachhead for Christianity among the Hurons. "I looked with tenderness and emotion on the place where we had lived, and where we had celebrated the Holy Sacrifice of the Mass through three years." He walked among the ruins, and nostalgic memories came to him.

Evening was near. He found a path, and bewildered and anxious, he groped his way through the gloomy forest. He came to a clearing, and there he saw the Indian village of Ihonatiria.

They saw him, robed in black, only his face and hands showing, as he emerged from the forest, tall, powerful, impressive. "Echon has come back!" they cried, running to meet him. "Echon has come again!" they shouted joyously as they swarmed about him. It was a heart-warming welcome for the missionary, and his feelings welled up in gratitude to God and to these spiritual children of his.

He rested briefly, then set out with some young braves to find his baggage. They returned with it an hour after midnight, and Brébeuf accepted the hospitality of Awandoay, a friendly, generous brave whose cabin was unusually large and well-stocked with beans and corn.

In the days that ensued, Brébeuf reestablished his place in the hearts of the Hurons, while he anxiously awaited the arrival of his Jesuit companions and the workmen. One by one they came, first Father Daniel in a state of exhaustion, then Davost, who had managed to make his way from the Island of the Allumettes and was half-dead from starvation and fatigue. The workmen came, each with his tale of hardship and privation, and so at last they were all there, assembled under the hospitable and ample roof of Awandoay. Once more the mission to the Hurons was begun.

Brébeuf selected a suitable site and drew plans for a cabin thirty-six feet long and twenty wide, divided into three sections. The Indians helped the French workers, and before October it was completed. It was after the Huron pattern, with its opening in the roof to allow the smoke to escape; but the division into rooms, and the doors, which swung on hinges, fascinated the people. They swarmed into the house at all hours and gaped at the wonders that Brébeuf had laid out for them to see. They were alarmed by the magnifying glass, which made the bugs in their hair seem like lobsters, and the mirror with many angles, which multiplied their noses, eyes, and ears. The magnet was pure magic and must have some sort of glue on it. But it was the clock that astounded them. They listened spellbound as it ticked and were stupefied when it chimed the hours. They thought it was alive and inquired what it ate. As the last stroke of the hour sounded, one of the Frenchmen would cry, "Stop!" and it obeyed.

"What does Captain Clock say?" they asked, when the clock struck.

"When he strikes twelve times," replied one of the Frenchmen, "he says, 'Hang on the kettle,' and when he strikes four times, he says, 'Get up and go home.' "

"All this," observes Brébeuf, "serves to gain their affection and make them more docile in respect to the admirable and incomprehensible mysteries of our Faith; for the opinion they have of our genius and capacity makes them believe whatever we tell them."

The orders of Captain Clock were well remembered. Visitors were always on hand to share the Fathers' sagamité, or bread, and on the stroke of four, all rose and departed, leaving the missionaries in peace for a time. The priests would bar the door, gather about the fire, and discuss the affairs of the mission. New words and expressions of the Hurons that each had noted were brought to the attention of all; new problems were discussed, new solutions arrived at. Then, repairing to their primitive chapel, conscious always that the efficacy of their labors depended upon close union with God through prayer, sacrifice, and love, they would perform their religious exercises with care and devotion.

Their orderly spiritual regimen is recounted by a Jesuit who later joined this mission in Ihonatiria, Father François du Péron:

> The importunity of the savages, who are continually about us in our cabin, and who sometimes break down a door, throw stones at our cabin, and wound our people — this importunity, I say, does not prevent our observance of our hours, as well regulated as in one of our colleges in France. At four o'clock the rising bell rings; then follows the orison, at the end of which the Masses begin and continue until eight o'clock; during this period each one keeps silent, reads his spiritual book, and says his lesser hours. At eight o'clock the door is left open to the savages, until four in the evening; it is permitted to talk with the savages at this time, as much to instruct them as to learn their language. In this time, also, our Fathers visit the cabins of the town, to baptize the sick and to instruct the well; as for me, my employment is the study of the language, watching the cabin, helping the Christians and catechumens pray to God, and keeping school for their children from noon until two o'clock, when the bell rings for examination of conscience. . . .
>
> At four o'clock in the evening, the savages who are not Christians are sent away, and we quietly say, all together, our matins and lauds, at the end of which we hold mutual

consultation for three-quarters of an hour about the advancement of and the hindrances to the Faith in these countries; afterward we confer together about the language until supper, which is at half-past six; at eight o'clock, the litanies, examination of conscience, and then we retire to sleep.

Father Jean de Brébeuf and his confreres visited the sick each day, comforting them and instructing them in the truths of the Christian Faith. As often as possible they gathered together the children of the village and sat them down in the cabin. Father Brébeuf would put on a surplice and biretta and chant the Our Father, which Father Daniel had translated into Huron rhymes, and the children would chant it after him. Next, he taught them the Sign of the Cross, the Hail Mary, the Apostles' Creed, and the Commandments. Briefly recalling the contents of the previous instruction, he would explain some new point in the Faith to the children, then question them upon their understanding of it. Two little French boys, who had been brought to Ihonatiria, would sum up the lesson and put questions to each other, a performance that filled the Indians with delight. When the session was over, Brébeuf would present them with a few beads, raisins, or prunes, and dismiss them.

Great rivalry in the Faith grew up among this small fry of Huronia. The youngsters would gather in groups about the village, vying with one another in making the Sign of the Cross or in chanting the rhymes they had learned, to the amusement and satisfaction of the priests.

On October 20 Brébeuf set out to visit the Petun, or Tobacco, Indians, a distinct nation of the Hurons. He was cheerfully greeted there, and he secured pledges of friendship. While with the Petuns, painstakingly preparing the way for other missionaries who might ultimately found missions among them, he baptized three sick children before they died.

He traveled through the January snows to Teanaustayé, the capital village of the Cord nation, another branch of the Hurons, where the Indians who had escorted him to Huronia the summer before lived. He wished to thank them for this, and to enlist the help of one of their number, Louis Amantacha, in planting the seeds of Christianity among his people. Louis was a Christian who had studied with the Récollet Fathers in France; he had escaped recently from the Iroquois, and Brébeuf felt that he could be helpful to the missionary effort. The chiefs of the Huron Federation were in Teanaustayé, consulting about peace with the Iroquois Senecas. In council they invited Brébeuf to accompany their delegation, but he was aware that treachery on one side or the other was possible, and he diplomatically declined, thinking it prudent not to become embroiled in tribal politics. Writing to Le Jeune, he said that if he went to the Senecas at all, he would go as an ambassador of Christ only.

Brébeuf returned to Ihonatiria, where he resumed his patient ministry among the Hurons. Not long after his arrival, a young brave, Oatii, being in poor health, asked for Baptism. He had been amply instructed in the Christian Faith, and the priest consented. He planned to create a fresh new impression in the minds of the villagers, and to this end he christened Oatii with particularly solemn rites in the chapel, bestowing upon him the name Joseph. The ceremony made a powerful impact upon the watching throng, and this was strengthened a few days later, on April 14, when Joseph's illness became critical, and Brébeuf administered the Sacrament of the Sick. This was the first time the sacrament had been given in Huronia. Joseph soon died, and Brébeuf conducted the full Catholic ritual when he was buried.

In that spring of 1635, a serious drought settled on the Huron country, bringing the customary panic into the hearts of the natives. Years before, at Toanché, the great Huron sorcerer Tehorenhaegnon had failed to bring rain, but the clouds had come and had opened up when Brébeuf and the Indians had honored the crucifix. Now again, in the nearby village of Andiatae, Tehorenhaegnon's incantations availed nothing, and again he asserted that Echon and the other Blackrobes were causing the drought by means of a demon housed in the cross above the mission cabin. The corn would rot, he said, and the people would starve unless the cross were taken down and destroyed. The warning swept the villages, and a swarm of Hurons whirled into Ihonatiria and demanded that the cross be taken down or they would burn the house to the ground.

Brébeuf faced the mob and asked them to attend a council that would be called by the chiefs of Ihonatiria. This was done, and he told the uneasy multitude, "It is not in the power of a Huron sorcerer or a French Blackrobe to bring rain when it is needed. That cross," he continued, "has been there for ten months; there has been rain and snow all winter; hence, it cannot be the cause of the drought. Hate sin, give up your superstitious practices, love God, serve Him and pray to Him with confidence, and He will hear you." He invited them to join him in a procession every day for nine days, and they agreed to do so.

That night the priests agreed that each would offer a novena of Masses in honor of St. Joseph. On June 5 the novena began. The priests offered their Masses each day, and each day the missionaries, the six Frenchmen, and the Hurons marched in solemn procession through the village, chanting prayers.

Eight of the nine days passed, and no rain had fallen. The ninth day opened clear and bright, and tension mounted. The procession formed and wound through the village streets. Clouds were gathering. Before they could reach the chapel again, the marchers were drenched in a torrent of rain.

Brébeuf was no less grateful than the Hurons. "These rains," he wrote, "stifled the false opinions and notions conceived against God, the cross, and ourselves. The savages . . . declared that in the future they would serve God. They uttered a thousand abusive words against their sorcerer [Tehorenhaegnon]. To God be forever the glory of the whole. He permits the dryness of the soil in order to bedew all hearts with His blessings."

Again, in late July, a drought endangered the corn crop, and the Indians appealed to Echon. He and his two companions responded with a novena of Masses in honor of the founder of the Society of Jesus, Ignatius Loyola, whose feast day was approaching. On the twenty-third of the month, which was the second day of the novena, as the priests and the Hurons were marching in procession chanting prayers, the heavens opened with a heavy downpour of rain, which saved the parched crops of corn.

Amid the distractions and alarms of life among the Indians, Brébeuf and his confreres carefully preserved the full vigor of their interior life. That summer they made their annual retreat of eight to ten days, following the Spiritual Exercises of St. Ignatius. "For these Spiritual Exercises," remarks Brébeuf, "we have so much more the need, since the sublimity of our labors requires so much the more a union with God, and since we are forced to live in continual turmoil. This makes us frequently realize that those who come here must bring a rich fund of virtue with them, if they wish here to gather the fruits thereof."

In addition to the spiritual exercises prescribed by the Society, Brébeuf performed many other devotions and penances, and was careful to do so in as great privacy as possible. "To the continual sufferings," wrote his spiritual director, "which are inseparable from the duties which he had in the missions, on the journeys, in whatever place he was; and to those which charity caused him to embrace, often above his strength, although below his courage, he added many voluntary mortifications. . . . And after all these, his heart could not be satiated with sufferings, and he believed that he had never endured aught."

On August 13 Brébeuf welcomed Father François Le Mercier, and four days later Father Pierre Pijart. These two Jesuits had come from Quebec to help advance the Huron mission. They handed him a letter from Champlain in which the governor addressed himself to the Hurons. In it, he repeated what he had told the Hurons who had come to Quebec that summer to trade. Brébeuf read the letter to the assembled Indians, whom Champlain counseled to love the Blackrobes and believe in God, to give no heed to the sorcerers but to listen to the Blackrobes. "The French will go in goodly numbers to your country," the letter read. "They will marry your daughters when they are baptized Christians. They will teach you to make hatchets and knives."

The Hurons who had just come from Quebec were amazed to hear Echon read to them the very words they had heard Champlain speak. How, they wondered, could Echon hear with his eyes the words which Champlain had spoken at a place thirty days' journey away?

"Next year," the letter went on, "you must bring some of your boys down to Quebec and leave them here for the winter. This will bind the Hurons and the French more closely together. Then, up in your own country, you must hold a great council of all the chiefs of the Ouendats [Wyandots] to consult on these matters. You must invite Echon to speak at that council."

Surely, thought the Hurons, Echon must be a great sorcerer.

During that fall and winter, Brébeuf regularly assembled the older Huron men in his cabin. He explained the existence of God to them and drew many illustrations from the laws of nature. He spoke to them about the Ten Commandments and how they must live if they truly believed in God and wished to enter Paradise.

The Hurons, Brébeuf reported, "acknowledged the Commandments to be very just and very reasonable. They thought these were matters of great importance, worthy of being discussed at the councils." They admitted the logic of his conclusions about God and His attributes. But, alas, "They know the beauty of the truth," he commented sadly; "they approve of it, but they do not embrace it. . . . They condemn their wicked customs, but when will they abandon them?" The step from belief to action was a long step, and they hesitated to pass from acknowledgment of God's existence to conformity with His laws.

Among the young, progress was more marked. Three little girls had mastered the catechism so thoroughly and gave such clear evidence of interior piety that Brébeuf and Daniel judged them ready for Baptism. Inviting the whole village to attend the ceremony, which took place on the feast of the Immaculate Conception, December 8, they performed the ritual with all possible solemnity. The chapel was thronged with Hurons when the three girls, beautifully appareled and ornamented with strings of wampum and porcelain, renounced Satan and all his works and received the waters of regeneration.

The Jesuit community that morning dedicated the Huron mission to the Immaculate Conception of the Blessed Virgin. They promised to offer twelve Masses in the ensuing year toward accomplishing in Huronia the erection of a permanent church named after the Immaculate Conception. "We believe," wrote

Brébeuf, "that the Blessed Virgin has accepted our humble devotions. Before the end of December we baptized twenty-eight."

The following year, 1636, was fruitful. Le Borgne, the treacherous chief of the Island of the Allumettes, visited Ihonatiria with new plots and departed unsuccessful but with thanks to Brébeuf for the priest's diplomatic consent to come to the island later on bearing gifts. The Iroquois were ranging Huronia and making hit-and-run attacks, and Brébeuf prevailed upon the Hurons to do away with their circular fortifications in favor of square palisades with defensive towers at each corner.

Amid all his duties, he wrote, at the request of Le Jeune, a comprehensive survey of all he had learned about the Hurons, an invaluable document for missionary purposes and to historians for three centuries; with it, he enclosed a booklet entitled "Directions for Priests of Our Society Who Shall Be Sent to the Hurons," setting out in close detail the requirements of character, deportment, courtesy, and method in laboring with these Indians. Finally, as superior of the Huron mission, he sent his official report to the general of the Society in Rome, wherein he reiterated, as in his booklet, the need for gentleness, patience, generosity, and example if one was to make true spiritual progress in Huronia.

Brébeuf received a long letter from Le Jeune that told the joyous news that eight ships had arrived with an abundance of supplies, hundreds of colonists, six priests, and two brothers. In partial counterbalance, Le Jeune related the sorrowful news of Champlain's death, and Brébeuf could do neither more nor less than concur in Le Jeune's tribute to this old friend: "Truly, he led a life of great justice, equity, and perfect loyalty to his King and toward the Gentlemen of the Company. But at his death, he crowned his virtues with sentiments of piety so lofty that he astonished us all."

On the evening of August 12, Brébeuf learned that a Blackrobe had just landed at the cove beneath Ihonatiria. He hurried down and came upon Father Pierre Chastellain, whom Aenon Indians had brought there. The next day, Father Charles Garnier arrived, and joy was unrestrained in Huronia.

That summer, Daniel and Davost traveled to Quebec. They took with them three Huron boys whom they planned to train as helpers in evangelizing their people. Twelve boys had originally promised to go, but maternal affection proved too strong. But with the three who persevered, a start could be made. Vice was still rampant among the Hurons, and the priests were bent on getting at least some of the youths into an environment where they would be protected against daily examples of profligacy. The Ursuline convent had effected such striking results with Indian girls that the missionaries thought to accomplish as much with the boys.

On September 2 Brébeuf baptized the first Iroquois ever to become a Christian. He was a Seneca chief whom the Hurons had captured and brought to Arontaen, a village about five miles from Ihonatiria. Brébeuf, anxious to save the soul of a man who was destined for burning at the stake, explained the truths of the Christian Faith, dwelling especially on the doctrine of offering up sufferings for the atonement of sins and for the happiness of Heaven. The captive was amazed that the missionaries should show such concern for his welfare, and he listened attentively. As Brébeuf instructed him, Garnier and Le Mercier prayed for him and vowed to offer up four Masses in honor of the Blessed Virgin if she should win him to Baptism. Finally he requested to be baptized, and this was done without hesitation, so well disposed had he proved himself.

The Huron chief had not decided whether to adopt him or kill him, and the captive was feasted for two days; it was then decreed that he should be tortured and burned. On September 4 the victim held his farewell feast and, as the host, offered to his captors the food that had been given him. While they gorged themselves, he kept shouting, "My brothers, I am about to die. Amuse yourselves boldly with me. I fear neither your tortures nor death." He sang songs of defiance and danced up and down while the Hurons applauded.

Eleven fires were kindled that night in the longhouse of the war chief. As soon as the prisoner was led in, braves pounced on him like tigers, tearing at him, beating him, pursuing him with flaming torches as he ran wildly from one end to the other. They would often stop him to break the bones of his hands; some pierced his ears with sharp sticks and bound his wrists with cords, which they pulled on with all their strength. At one point he fell, and the elders, fearful he might die that night, stopped the tortures, only to resume them when he revived. At intervals they would desist to give him water and corn, and on these occasions Brébeuf was able to come near the captive to console him.

The Hurons could not understand his solicitude for the prisoner. "Do you think," one of them asked, "that because of what you say and do now to this Iroquois, the Iroquois will treat you better if sometime they come to ravage our country?"

"That is not what concerns me," replied Brébeuf. "All I think of now is to do what I ought. We have come here only to teach you the way to Heaven. In regard to ourselves, we leave that entirely to the Providence of God."

The Iroquois was alive at dawn. They led him outside the village and tied him to a post on a scaffolding six feet high. They seared him with torches and thrust these down his throat and into his fundament. They fastened red-hot hatchets about his shoulders and burned his eyes. They cut off a foot, then a hand, and finally severed the head from the shoulders. The trunk was dismembered and put into kettles, and the Indians ate with relish the flesh of an Iroquois.

As the missionaries walked home after the slaughter, the shrieks of the Seneca chief rang in their ears and the specter of his tormented body stood before their eyes. They offered up their Masses on the next morning for the repose of the soul of the first Seneca and the first Iroquois to die a Christian.

There now were enough priests and lay helpers[14] at Ihonatiria to extend the missionary enterprise, and with fresh hope and enthusiasm, the priests formulated their plans to this end. The long-projected crusade to plant the Cross in every village was about to get under way. The Fathers discussed the aspects of forthcoming ventures one evening, and joined together in prayer that these might be accomplished to the greater glory of God. They lay on their humble cots in a condition of excitement, for the Huron mission was out of its swaddling clothes at last and was about to stride forward.

---

[14]Six priests, including Jogues, and at least five lay helpers.

~

Chapter 8

Events took a sudden and unexpected turn. Three of the new-comers had scarcely gotten settled when they were attacked by a contagious fever, apparently a virulent form of pneumonia, which turned their mission house into a hospital. Two of the lay helpers were soon prostrated. Medicine was lacking, and the patients grew weaker until they seemed on the point of death. Slowly they recovered, only to be confronted with a new calamity.

The pestilence that for two years had visited the Huron settlements from time to time broke out now with tenfold violence. With it appeared the even more dreaded smallpox. Both maladies raged through the fall and, instead of abating when winter came, reached new fury. Terror mounted to panic and hysteria throughout Huronia. Huddled together in their cabins, with no segregation of those stricken, the natives fell easy victims.

The missionaries, singly or in pairs, trekked tirelessly through snow and ice from village to village, ministering to the sick, speaking words of comfort, inviting them to say a few simple prayers, and doing all in their power to relieve their sufferings. They left a few raisins, a prune, and a spoonful of sweetened water with the sufferers. When they were able to make a little broth, they distrib-uted this among the grateful patients.

Thousands of Hurons lay writhing in pain. Hundreds were dragged dead from their huts, and not a family escaped. Scarcely a household in Huronia went unvisited by the missionaries. Hav-ing done what they could to relieve the Indians' bodily distress, they would tell them briefly of God and of His divine Son, who re-deemed the world and instituted sacraments to channel His grace to men.

They would say a few words about Heaven and Hell and urge the individual to offer his sufferings to God in atonement for past sins. In many instances, the Indian would remain stolidly silent; sometimes he would be evasive, intractable, or uninterested in the white man's Paradise.

"I wish to go where my relatives and ancestors have gone," was a common reply.

"Heaven is a good place for Frenchmen," others would say, "but I wish to be among Indians, for the French will give me nothing to eat when I get there."

"Which will you choose," asked a missionary of a dying woman, "Heaven or Hell?"

"Hell," she replied, "if my children are there."

When the priests succeeded in clearing away misconceptions and eliciting faith and contrition, they would pour a little water from a cup or the hollow of the hand as they pronounced the words of Baptism.

During the epidemic, the missionaries baptized more than twelve hundred persons. In one village, where the people were the most perverse, some were anxious to follow Christian instruction, and in the end about a hundred were baptized, including twenty-two children.

The natives of the village of Wenrio, having tried all the rites and dances prescribed by their medicine men, invited the Black-robes to a council.

"What must we do," asked the chief, "that your God may take pity on us?"

"You must believe in Him," replied Brébeuf. "Keep His Commandments; abjure your faith in dreams; take but one wife and be true to her; give up your superstitious feasts; renounce your assemblies of debauchery; eat no human flesh; never give feasts to demons, and make a vow that, if God will deliver you from this pest, you will build a chapel to offer Him thanksgiving and praise."

The terms seemed hard to the natives, and they tried to settle by offering only to build the chapel. Father Brébeuf refused to compromise, and the council broke up.

The Jesuits, ill-clad and undernourished, with unwearying patience trudged from village to village to bring physical comfort and spiritual solace to the desolated Indians.

"When we see them," writes Francis Parkman, "in the gloomy February of 1637, and the gloomier months that followed, toiling on foot from one infected town to another, wading through the sodden snow, under the bare and dripping forests, drenched with incessant rains, till they descried at length through the storm the clustered dwellings of some barbarous hamlet — when we see them entering, one after another, these wretched abodes of misery and darkness, and all for one sole end, the baptism of the sick and dying, we may smile at the futility of the object, but we must needs admire the self-sacrificing zeal with which it was pursued."[15] Parkman, with his casual attitude toward Baptism, would find eternal folly in the words of Brébeuf, so often stated: "I

<hr>

[15] Parkman, *The Jesuits in North America*, 98.

would go to the ends of the earth to bring Baptism to a single savage."

It was a busy time for the Huron sorcerers. They prescribed one preposterous remedy after another. Arrows were shot at the moon; drums were beaten; they sang and shouted until they were hoarse and pursued their weird and obscene dances until they fell frothing, hysterical, and exhausted. When all their prescriptions accomplished nothing, the medicine men turned one by one with malignant vengeance upon the Blackrobes. "They are the cause of the plague," they said. "They seek to destroy the whole Huron nation. Although thousands of our people have died, not a single Frenchman has passed away. Note that nearly all whom the Blackrobes have baptized have perished. Only when they are killed will the spirits end the plague."

The Hurons, having tried all else and failed, considered the new remedy proposed by their sorcerers. The thousand acts of kindness were forgotten; the charges against the missionaries echoed from village to village. The Indians scowled at them wherever they went, and many barred their cabins against them. As the threats became more overt, the Fathers wondered when some hotheaded brave would plunge a tomahawk into their skulls. A council was called, and the decision was made.

Brébeuf wrote to his superior in Quebec, dating his letter October 28, 1637, from Ossossané:

We are perhaps upon the point of shedding our blood in the service of our Good Master, Jesus Christ. . . . I assure you that all our priests await the outcome of this matter with great calmness and serenity of soul. As for myself, I can say to your Reverence, with all sincerity, that I have not yet had the slightest dread of death from such a cause. But we are all grieved over this, that these poor barbarians, through their own malice, are closing the door to the gospel and to grace.

Whatever conclusion they reach, and whatever treatment they accord us, we will try, by the grace of our Lord, to endure it patiently for His service. It is a singular favor that His goodness gives us, to allow us to endure something for love of Him. Now it is that we consider ourselves as belonging truly to the Society. May He be forever blessed for having chosen us, from among so many others better than we and destined for this country, to aid Him in bearing His Cross.

That afternoon Brébeuf sent criers through Ossossané to announce that he was holding his farewell feast, which Indian etiquette prescribed should be given by those about to die. Hungry natives crowded into his cabin. When they had all satisfied their voracious appetites, Brébeuf arose to speak. He did not extol his prowess nor defy their tortures as the Indians did; he spoke to them about God, His love, Heaven, and Hell. They listened silently; the customary grunts of approval were conspicuously lacking. Moodily they withdrew. The stage was set.

But a lull in the general anger came. Sticks and stones were occasionally thrown at the missionaries, tomahawks were brandished over their heads, but they were not seriously molested. Gradually they were allowed to enter the cabins and resume their labors of mercy. Threatened sentences of torture and death were not executed. It is probable that the older heads had convinced the angry ones that to carry out the executions would end by arraying against the Hurons another enemy besides the Iroquois — namely, the French. These would shift their trading to another

Indian nation, and they would also take vengeance on the Hurons. In their present state of weakness, menaced increasingly by Iroquois attacks, the Hurons could not afford to create new and powerful enemies.

By the following year, the fears of the natives became almost completely dissipated. Their affection for the priests was restored to such a degree that it was possible now to erect a permanent missionary establishment in the village of Teanaustayé, which had been particularly hostile to the missionaries. On June 25, 1638, Brébeuf and his confreres departed from Ihonatiria, whose population had been drastically reduced by the plague, and moved into their new mission. This they called Saint Joseph's II, the first at Ihonatiria having been named after that patron saint of the Huron missions.

Father Jerome Lalemant arrived the next August. He was the younger brother of Charles Lalemant, who had come to Quebec in 1625 with Brébeuf and Massé. Brébeuf was overjoyed to learn that Father Jerome was to supplant him as superior of the Huron mission. But his feelings were not fully shared by the other missionaries, for they loved and revered Brébeuf and held him to be the outstanding Jesuit missionary in all of New France. They had been daily witnesses to his piety, his austerities, his prayer prolonged far into the night in the blackness of the chapel, and his unfailing kindness and selfless zeal. They valued especially his equanimity of temper, so important in a mission where vexations were daily and even hourly visitors.

"His evenness of temper," wrote his later superior, Father Ragueneau, "seemed to be the virtue that outweighed all others. Nothing could upset him. During the twelve years I have known him, whether as superior or subject, I never saw him angry or even slightly indignant."

Father Jerome Lalemant had proved himself an able adminis-
trator in France. He had read all the *Relations* sent by Le Jeune and
Brébeuf, and he had learned much about the Huron mission from
his brother Charles.

His first concern was to erect a large, permanent central residence, upon which all other missions in the area would depend.
This plan was prompted by the Indian custom of abandoning their
villages every ten or twenty years, when the soil became depleted,
so forcing the Jesuits to abandon their cabins and churches and
build new ones. Moreover, the missionaries required an adequate
center where they could recuperate when ill, make spiritual retreats, and give refuge to persecuted Huron Christians. Accordingly, Sainte Marie was erected, with its chapel, guest house,
residence, and strong fortifications.

From this impregnable center Father Lalemant sent forth his
thirteen missionaries throughout all Huronia and to other tribes.
In 1640 he commissioned Charles Garnier and Pierre Pijart to
preach the gospel to the Petuns, and Brébeuf and Joseph Chaumonot
to preach to the Neutrals.

The Neutrals were a tribe of about twelve thousand, distributed among forty villages. They occupied the territory immediately north of Lake Erie and a wing of land extending between that
lake and Lake Ontario, across the Niagara River, and into what is
now western New York. Their Indian name was Ottiwandaronk,
they spoke a language cognate to the Iroquois, and they were
called Neutrals because they declined to take sides in the wars between Iroquois and Huron. Taller and more shapely than the Hurons, they were surpassed by no other Indian tribe in athletic
proportions, ferocity, and extravagance of superstition. The Hurons would not torture a woman at the stake, but the Neutrals felt
no inhibitions in this respect.

The Neutrals carried to preposterous extremes the Indian notion that madness endows a person with mysterious and super-human powers. In consequence, their country abounded in pre-tended maniacs who raved stark naked through the villages, scattering brands from the cabin fires and upsetting everything in their path. Madness was frequently assumed as a pretext for every manner of license, robbery, and murder.

When a member of the tribe died, the Neutrals would not carry off the corpse immediately, as the Hurons did, but would let it rot in the wigwam until their calloused nostrils could no longer en-dure the stench.

It was to such people that Brébeuf and Chaumonot turned their steps on November 2, 1640. At Saint Joseph they secured a guide, and after five days of wilderness travel, they reached the first Neutral town. To their intense chagrin, they learned that two Huron emissaries had preceded them, denouncing them as evil sorcerers bent on exterminating the Indians. These Hurons had presented the Neutrals with a gift of nine French hatchets on con-dition that they put the Blackrobes to death. Little wonder that when Brébeuf and Chaumonot appeared, they heard cries of "Flee! Echon the demon is coming!" Women and children made off, and the men kept sullenly aloof.

The missionaries could only guess the reason for this perfor-mance. Possibly the mischievous Hurons thought this a conve-nient way of having Brébeuf executed without incurring the enmity of the French. In this manner, the blame would fall upon the Neutrals, while the Hurons could present themselves at Que-bec the following summer in a condition of apparent innocence and with profuse expressions of sorrow.

The Neutrals lost little time calling a council to decide the fate of the Blackrobes. The priests, although uninvited, appeared before the council and offered a wampum belt of two thousand porcelain beads as a token of friendship. It was refused, on the pretext that the chief was absent. Brébeuf sensed the ominous significance of such a refusal, and with Chaumonot he withdrew.

The deliberations lasted until midnight. Three times the death sentence was passed, but the influence of some of the older chiefs deferred its execution. One of the Indians, who had given shelter for the night to the missionaries, returned to his cabin to tell them what had transpired. He was astonished to find them fast asleep on the floor. They had lived under threat of death so many times that it had ceased to disquiet them, and a good conscience provided them with a defense against nervous anxiety.

The Jesuits were safe for the time being, but the Neutrals agreed that henceforth none should give them shelter. They tramped from village to village, breasting the heavy snows and forest underbrush, only to find that the inhabitants had been alerted against them. Half-starved, half-frozen, endeavoring doggedly to bring to the savages the good tidings of man's redemption, they were driven from every door, struck, and spat upon by pretended maniacs.

One day, in the forest depths, Brébeuf saw in a vision a great cross; its stem stood in the heart of the Iroquois country and its arms overshadowed Huronia. "The cross was large enough," related Jean, "to bear all the missionaries among the Hurons." In his spiritual notes Brébeuf relates that when, on the night of February 8, he was in prayer, "striving to conform myself to the Divine Will and . . . saying, 'May Thy will be done, O Lord,' I heard a voice saying to me, 'Take up and read.' When morning came, I took in my hand that small golden book of *The Imitation of Christ* and happened upon the chapter on 'The Royal Way to the Holy Cross.' From this there followed in my soul a great peace and quiet in the things that chanced to happen."

Saints of the American Wilderness

They pushed on until they reached Onquiara, a village near Niagara Falls, and from there they journeyed to another settlement that came near being their grave. Late at night, trudging through deep snow in a clear cold that was splitting the trees, they spied a miserable cluster of huts. Growing faint with exhaustion and in grave danger of freezing to death, they determined to force their way into a cabin even at the risk of being tomahawked.

They crouched before the door of a cabin and waited for someone to come out. Presently the deerskin was pushed aside and a brave emerged. They rushed in before he could stop them. The inmates, aghast at their boldness, were infuriated, but once the travelers were inside, the Indian law of hospitality forbade their being harmed. Even so, the young men were restrained only with difficulty from tomahawking them on the spot.

"Go out and leave our country," cried an old chief, "or we will put you into the kettle and make a feast of you."

To this, a young brave added, "I have had enough of the dark-colored flesh of our enemies. I wish to know the taste of white meat, and I will eat yours."

Suddenly a warrior rushed in like a maniac, drew his bow, and aimed the arrow at Chaumonot. "I looked at him fixedly," relates the missionary, "and commended myself in full confidence to Saint Michael. Without doubt this great archangel saved us; for almost immediately the fury of the warrior was appeased, and the rest of our enemies soon began to listen to the explanation we gave them of our visit to their country."

In view of the mood that prevailed among the Neutrals, Brébeuf and Chaumonot realized that to continue their present efforts would only incite further bitterness. They decided to return to Sainte Marie, and they headed off into the wintry forestland. A heavy, swirling blizzard obliged them to seek shelter in the village of Teotondiaton, where a kindly squaw took them into her cabin. She befriended them, acted like a mother toward them, and extended every form of hospitality during the twenty-five days of their enforced stay.

This good-hearted squaw helped the missionaries compile a vocabulary of the Neutral language, dictating the words slowly and clearly, syllable by syllable. To have accomplished this was a wonder; but added to it was their further achievement of writing a book on the comparative philology of the Huron and Neutral dialects, which, according to Father Jerome Lalemant, was worth spending years of exile to complete. He regarded the delay of the two Fathers there as "an exceptional providence of God." It is one of the glories of Caesar that he wrote his famous *Commentaries* in the very midst of war's alarms; in every way comparable was the performance of these two ragged, weary, half-frozen men, laboring in a squalid, snowbound hut amid scuffling children, barking dogs, intrusive and garrulous Indians, the antics of real or pretended maniacs, and a perpetual cloud of acrid smoke that caused their eyes to inflame.

While returning to Sainte Marie with Chaumonot and four other missionaries who had joined them on the way, Brébeuf fell on the ice and broke his collarbone. The pain was intense, and he could not lift his left arm. His companions strapped the arm to his side and suggested that a sled be made to carry him over the trails. Declaring he was still able to use his legs, Brébeuf turned down the proposal, and they continued on. They cleared places in the snow and passed the nights there, while the wind blustered and the cold pierced the marrow. Brébeuf at one point confided to Chaumonot that the pain was severe, but no greater than the agony he had asked from God. "We proceeded joyously and with courage," wrote Chaumonot, "despite the cold, the fatigue, and countless falls on the ice."

Their goal was not only to reach Sainte Marie, but to reach it by March 19, the feast of Saint Joseph, to whom they anxiously wished to offer Masses. They fasted from midnight and arose with the dawn. They weathered the sodden snow, the muddy, slushy paths, and the swollen streams. Limp and exhausted, they straggled into Sainte Marie a few minutes before noon on the nineteenth. Waving off the customary welcome, they washed, confessed, and hurried to the altars, where the missals already were open at the Mass of Saint Joseph. This was their first opportunity to receive Holy Communion since November 2, four and a half months before.

That evening the results of Brébeuf and Chaumonot's months of labor and unending disappointment were reviewed. They had not established a mission among the Neutrals; they had not won a single convert. But, for all that, they had not failed. They had accumulated valuable information concerning the location of the Neutral villages and the temper and manner of the people. They had insinuated into some of the Indians' minds an idea of God, of Christ the Redeemer, and of the afterlife. Too, they had exposed the natives to the Christian character as exemplified in the two missionaries themselves. They had made a beginning, and Lalement remarked that "even if this evangelizing of the Indians is not accomplished until shortly before the end of the world, yet it is always necessary to begin before the ending."

Jean de Brébeuf had been in the Indian wilderness for seven consecutive years, enduring hardship and every opportunity for Christian humility and longsuffering. His powerful constitution had been taxed to the limit. Now he needed medical care, for his fracture was slow to heal and the pain was extreme. On May 20 he was sent to Quebec to recuperate and to give the superior, Father Vimont, and Governor Montmagny a comprehensive report on the mission and the state of the Indians. His canoe slid into the little river of Sainte Marie and breasted its choppy waters. The veteran missionary looked back to the forested headlands above Ihonatiria and the abandoned village of Toanché, which he had first glimpsed fifteen years before.

At Quebec he ministered to the French and the Indians, as well as at the settlement of Sillery not far distant, and he visited the sick at the Hotel-Dieu, a hospital conducted by the Ursuline nuns. He heard sad news of Huronia, where the roving Iroquois, aroused to furious pitch and equipped with firearms sold to them by the Dutch, were taking heavy toll among their age-long enemies. Surely, unless measures were taken to halt them, they would annihilate the Hurons, who were armed for the most part with tomahawk and bow and arrow.

Brébeuf's heart was in Huronia and, recovered, thither he went, setting forth in the first week of August 1644 with two young Jesuit priests, Chabanel and Garreau. This was his third mission to the Hurons, and his heart bounded with joy. As he stepped into the canoe, he prayed that God would accept his vow of eleven years before, which he had repeated each day since then at the altar: to give his life, if occasion required, for the Faith of Christ.

He was back at Sainte Marie on September 7, 1644, and at once he plunged into his missionary labors. He took opportunities also to deepen and intensify his own interior life, and he tells of a vision that came to him on October 8. In this, he saw himself and his companions wearing garments stained with blood. Fortified with ever-freshening spiritual strength, single-minded in his fierce dedication to bring Christ to the Indians, he went forth from the central bastion of Sainte Marie and ministered to the neighboring villages of the Huron Ataronchronons — St. Louis, St. Anne, St.

Jean, St. Denis, St. Xavier. Month after month this strong, gentle, fervent, courteous Jesuit priest trekked increasingly well-worn paths from place to place, instructing, baptizing, and consoling.

A year went by since he had last embarked at Quebec, and in August 1645, he made his annual retreat. In his spiritual notebook he recorded that "every day from now on, at the time of Communion, with the consent of the superior, I will vow that I will do whatever I shall know to be for the greater glory of God and for His greater service."

Father Paul Ragueneau had come to Sainte Marie as superior, and of Brébeuf he wrote, "He derived his spirit of confidence in God from prayer, in which he was often much uplifted. . . . At one time, I find in his writing that, while he was in prayer, God detached him from all his senses and united him to Himself; again, that he was enraptured in God, and fervently embraced Him; at other times, he says that his whole heart was transported to God by bursts of love which were ecstatic. But above all, this love was tender with respect to the sacred person of Jesus Christ, and of Jesus Christ suffering."

Sainte Marie had an unexpected visitor in September of that year: the Jesuit Father Francis Bressani, who had been tortured by the Iroquois in April 1644. He had been ransomed by the Dutch and sent by them to France. This summer he had come back to Quebec and rejoined the missions. Brébeuf gazed with reverence at the scars on Bressani's face, neck, legs, and arms and observed that some of his fingers were missing, while others had been chewed to stubs. A Christian Huron was present, and he remarked, "If there were not a Paradise, could there be found men who would walk through the fires and the flames of the Iroquois in order to draw us from Hell and lead us to Heaven?" Ragueneau said, expressing the mind of the missionaries, "His mutilated hands have made him a better preacher than we, and have served more than all our tongues to give a better conception than ever of the truths of our Faith to our Huron Christians."

That November, Brébeuf made a journey into the country of the Nipissings to look after some Christian Hurons who had taken refuge with them through fear of the wide-ranging Iroquois. He found "in the midst of those profound forests and vast solitudes a whole family of Christians who adored God in those woods, who lived there in innocence, and who received him and his comrade as guests who had been sent from Heaven."

~

Chapter 9

In September 1648, Sainte Marie welcomed a Jesuit missionary whose days of service to the Hurons were to be the shortest among all the martyrs of the Society. He was to be associated intimately with Jean de Brébeuf, whose service was longest, and the climax of his dedication was to be Brébeuf's climax also.

Gabriel Lalemant was the third of that family name to cast his lot with the missions of New France. His uncle Charles had come there with Brébeuf in 1625, and his uncle Jerome was the first superior of Sainte Marie, which he had founded. Gabriel was physically a weakling beside the burly Brébeuf, but in moral courage he did not compare unfavorably.

Gabriel was born in Paris on October 31, 1610, the youngest of six children. All these but one entered the religious life: Bruno, the eldest, joined the Carthusians; the second son became a distinguished jurist; two daughters entered the Convent of the Assumption in Paris, and the third was a Carmelite. The father died when Gabriel was young, but the mother kept her family intact and saw them to their respective goals. Later, when news of Gabriel's martyrdom reached them, his Carmelite sister knelt down and recited the *Magnificat,* and his mother consecrated herself as a cloistered nun.

At nineteen, Gabriel bade his mother farewell and entered the Jesuit novitiate on March 24, 1630. In the midst of her tears at parting, she said, "I give you up, Gabriel, dear as you are to me, that you may devote your life to God as a member of the Society of Jesus. Serve Him faithfully all the days of your life, and we shall be united again, in Heaven."

Years later, grateful to his family, most particularly to his mother, for a childhood and youth of rare happiness and love, he wrote in his spiritual diary, "I am indebted to my family, and I must draw upon them the effects of God's mercies. My God, never permit that any of this family for which You have had so much love shall perish in Your sight, or be numbered among those who are destined to blaspheme You eternally. Let me be the victim for them."

After his two years' novitiate, Gabriel taught at the Jesuit college at Moulins. Three years later, he was studying theology at Bourges, and in 1638 he was ordained to the priesthood. The following year he was appointed to the staff of the College of La Flèche, and in 1641 the Society sent him to Moulins to teach philosophy.

At this time, there was tremendous interest in the missions of New France. As the volumes of the *Relations* were issued annually, they became bestsellers. A whole new and exciting world of Indians, forest land, and intrepid missionaries was opening before the eyes of the French. Gabriel, whose own two uncles were there, grew avid for service in the missions, and for this he prayed long and fervently and petitioned his superiors repeatedly. He was always rejected because of his frail constitution and uncertain health.

Undismayed, he persevered in his prayers and in his requests, confident that God would grant him this burning wish. Finally, in the spring of 1646, Father Etienne Charlet, the Jesuit superior in

France, gave his reluctant consent. "Father Gabriel Lalemant had come last to the war," wrote the battle-scarred missionary Bressani, "and gained the victory among the first. He had asked God for this grace during many years; and having obtained it from Him, it could not be denied him by the superiors — although he was of an extremely frail constitution and almost without other strength than what his zeal and fervor supplied him."

On September 20, 1646, Gabriel was welcomed at Quebec by his uncle Jerome Lalemant. He handed over to Jerome and the other priests the messages and letters from France with which he had been laden, and he was granted a brief rest from the rigors of the sea voyage. He was assigned to minister to the French colonists in Quebec, Sillery, Beauport, and Three Rivers, and while so occupied, he took every opportunity to study the Indian languages and the customs and beliefs of the Indians. Gabriel never lost sight of his primary objective, the Huron missions, and after two years, he repeated to his uncle the request he had earnestly made upon his arrival at Quebec, that he should be sent west.

"It is unfortunate," his uncle replied, "that so brave a spirit is clothed in a body so frail, that a soul so strong is handicapped by a body so weak. But the life among the savages is so primitive as to tax the strength of our strongest missionaries. It would not be prudent to send you to the Hurons, where the physical hardships are so great."

"God will give me the strength, Father Superior," replied Gabriel, "'and in Him I can do all things.'"

Faith moves mountains, and prayer changes the will of men. Father Gabriel had won out again. On July 24, 1648, he departed Quebec for Three Rivers, where he would await the Hurons. There were four new missionaries in the party that slipped out from that trading post on August 6 in a flotilla of sixty Huron canoes. There were also twenty-six French laborers and soldiers, and the veteran Father Bressani was the leader.

Over the thousand miles of river and woodland portage, the young Gabriel learned firsthand of the tough Indian life. He ate the watery cornmeal, slept in the open, and helped carry the baggage, and to the surprise of the Indians, he exulted in these hardships for which he had yearned.

And so, early in September, he was greeted by the Fathers at Sainte Marie. He was delighted to observe the fidelity with which the Jesuit missionaries in this remote wilderness observed the order of their religious exercises; it was almost as though he were stepping into a house of the Society in France. During his few days' rest there, Gabriel briefed himself on the work of the mission and his own imminent duties.

Sainte Marie was well staffed, he learned, but so far and so often had the missionaries to travel that it was rare to find more than two or three priests together there. Sometimes only one priest was present to say Mass for the numerous lay helpers and to assist the visiting Indians in their religious obligations. The missionaries were able to evangelize most profitably during the winter months, because the Hurons were in their villages, easily reached, while in summer they were off tilling the soil or hunting and fishing. The country was dotted with small Indian settlements, and because a missionary frequently had to take charge of as many as ten or twelve groups of catechumens, he was constantly flitting from place to place. Others were away in more distant parts — among the Petuns beyond the Blue Hills, among the Algonquins around Lake Nipissing — and they would remain there for months.

A few days after his arrival, Gabriel Lalemant was sent to the mission at Ossossané and there, under the tutelage of Chaumonot, he commenced to make incredible progress in the Huron tongue and revealed a singular aptitude for missionary work. When January 1649 was at hand, he became assistant to Jean de Brébeuf, of whose accomplishments he had heard and read so much. His delight knew no bounds. A few short years ago, he had seemed consigned to making the rounds of the Jesuit colleges in France; now he was companion to the giant of the Huron missions. With this personality he would advance rapidly in the language of the Hurons, and he would master the art of promoting their spiritual advancement. At the side of his tall comrade, he soon was trudging through the snow, taking his turn at pulling the sled, which was "laden with their little goods and chattels, through narrow paths covered with snow which, frequently disappearing, left the travelers in doubt and uncertainty as to the way they should go."

Gabriel confided to Brébeuf that he had sought two favors from God: to be a Jesuit and, if possible, to die for Christ. The first had been granted, and he hoped fervently the second would not be denied him. The aspiration of this youthful missionary touched the veteran priest, who confided in turn that he, too, had offered himself to God, body and soul, and had begged of God the opportunity of shedding his blood to further the spiritual conquest of the Indians.

At the outset, the schedule of Brébeuf and Lalemant prescribed that they start off on Monday to make the rounds of their half-dozen villages. They would baptize, hear confessions, say Mass, give instructions, and visit the sick. They were to be back on Saturday to take care of their own villagers at Sainte Marie, and of the Hurons who came there from far and near to assist at Mass. It had long been a profound satisfaction to the missionaries "to see," in the words of Father Ragueneau, "arriving here from two, three, and four leagues' distance on Saturday evenings a number of our Christians, who camp near our residence in order to celebrate the Sundays with us. Many Algonquins wintered near us this year, and it was a sweet anthem to hear the praises of God sung in three or four different languages at the same time. This house is a house of peace, so much so that the very Indians who elsewhere are most hostile and most insolent toward us assume a feeling and disposition wholly different when they see us in our own home.

"During the past year, we counted over three thousand persons to whom we gave shelter, and sometimes within a fortnight to six or seven hundred Christians, which, as a rule, means three meals to each one. This does not include a larger number who came continually to pass a whole day, and to whom we also gave charity; so that in a strange country we feed those who themselves should supply us with the necessaries of life."

Gabriel Lalemant and his tutor-companion Jean de Brébeuf made their profitable rounds and through winter storms kept manfully to their timetable of mercy. Monday they set forth, during the week they ministered to the mission villages, and on Saturday they were back at Sainte Marie. Edified by the veteran's zeal, the younger man grew in spiritual stature and advanced in his chosen work. The stringencies of travel and of the rough life among the Hurons did not hinder him or Brébeuf from intensifying that interior perfection of the soul which is the principal ingredient of active apostleship.

~

The Iroquois were progressively increasing their forays. Toward the end of 1648, a party of three hundred Huron men and women, mostly Christians, had encamped in the woods. A large band of Senecas swooped down upon them, massacred most, and carried the rest into captivity. Soon after, the dead were being buried by nearby Hurons, and these were slaughtered by an Iroquois war party that poured out from the forest.

The missionaries were profoundly alarmed, for they were not unaware that total disaster might be afoot for the Huron nation. A few weeks after this twin disaster, Brébeuf decided in the light of continuing threats to the Hurons to change the location of the poorly protected village of St. Ignace, which was one of the mission settlements visited weekly by Brébeuf and Lalemant. Together they chose an ideal site, which was protected on three sides by a deep ravine and could be strongly defended on the fourth. Under Brébeuf's direction, the Hurons constructed a heavy palisade wall fifteen feet high, and they laid in a good supply of bows and arrows and tomahawks.

In the second week of March 1649, in a world of soggy snow and sticky mud, the two missionaries visited the new St. Ignace during their round of the missions. They learned that hundreds of braves with their chiefs had fanned out into the forest to sweep it clear of the enemy, who were reported on the southern and eastern frontiers. Other braves were absent, trading with other nations. Four or five hundred Hurons remained, mostly old men, women, children, and the ailing.

The two priests, having performed their duties there, walked to the village of St. Louis, three miles away, where they spent a day or two about their tasks. On Friday of that week, they were back at Sainte Marie, where they spent Saturday and Sunday. Stephen Annaotaha, a renowned war chief from St. Louis, was present and made a general confession. He had a presentiment of danger, he said.

Monday morning, March 15, Brébeuf and Lalemant started out. They spent the day and night at St. Louis, and a little after dawn on Tuesday, they said their Masses. Three miles away, St. Ignace lay in peaceful sleep; the carelessly unbolted gate swung in the breeze, and no sentries patrolled the palisade platforms.

A small band of Iroquois threaded their way through the woods, slipping swiftly and silently from tree to tree, and headed toward the palisaded side of St. Ignace. They paused at the edge of the forest, and they perceived the open gate and the unguarded palisades. This reconnoitering band signaled the main body of one thousand warriors, mostly Senecas and Mohawks. In waves they swept upon the village, rushed with wild whoops into the cabins, and tomahawked the inhabitants before they could reach for bow and arrow. A few were taken captive. The work was accomplished in a few minutes.

Three Hurons escaped. Half-naked, stricken with terror, they fled to St. Louis, where Brébeuf and Lalemant were just finishing the prayers after Mass. The priests heard the dreaded cry, "The Iroquois! The Iroquois! They are at your gate!"

The seven hundred inhabitants of St. Louis were stricken with fear. Most of them fled in panic. Of the warriors, about eighty remained. Many of the old and sick were perforce left in their lodges. The braves, unaware of the enemy's strength, shouted defiance and, directed by Stephen Annaotaha, manned the palisades.

The two priests rose from their prayers and hurried out into the village. Stephen rushed up to them and exclaimed, "My brothers, save yourselves! Go now, while there is time!" Brébeuf and Lalemant knew they could escape, but they spurned the thought.

"No, Stephen," Brébeuf replied. "I am remaining to minister to my people to the end." Turning to his young companion, he encouraged him to flee. Lalemant begged for permission to stay, and Brébeuf acquiesced.

The Iroquois came. With whoops and shrieks, their faces smeared with the blood of their victims at St. Ignace, they threw themselves upon the palisades with the fury of tigers. Yell echoed yell, shot answered shot. The Hurons fought with abandon. Using arrows, stones, and a few guns, they killed thirty Iroquois and wounded many more.

Twice they repulsed the attackers, and the Iroquois came back each time with new ferocity. They swarmed about the palisades, chopping at them with their hatchets until at several points they cut through. Wild struggles ensued at these breaches.

Brébeuf and Lalemant shouted encouragement to the defenders. Bending over the wounded, they spoke to them, absolving some and baptizing others. They hurried into the cabins, aiding the sick and the women and children.

The Iroquois had overwhelmed the defenders at the breaches and were streaming through. They killed or captured the remaining Huron braves and swarmed into the cabins. They split the heads of those they found there and seized furs and other possessions. They hurled firebrands into the bark cabins, and what few living persons remained, unable to escape, died screaming in the flames.

The attackers fell upon Brébeuf and Lalemant, beat them, bound them fast, and led them with the other captives back to St. Ignace. When they reached the clearing before the wreckage of that village, the Iroquois stripped the priests stark naked and, in turn with the captured Hurons, made them run the gauntlet of sticks and clubs.

Shivering in their nakedness from the raw March winds, the priests were driven with the Hurons into the huge cabin that Brébeuf had designed in the hope that it would one day be a church. Fires were burning about six torture posts. Brébeuf and Lalemant managed to speak words of consolation to the huddled Hurons, urging them to offer their sufferings to God. Brébeuf told his companion that if the Iroquois should carry Gabriel to their own country as a prisoner, he should try to escape, as Bressani had done. Each missionary listened to the other in confession and raised his hand in absolution.

The Iroquois chose Brébeuf and some Hurons for the first tor-ments. Leaping upon him as he prayed, they broke the bones of his hands, tore out his fingernails, and munched on his fingers. When they dragged him to one of the posts, he embraced it and kissed it. Quickly they pulled back his arms and fastened his wrists to the post. They were determined to smash his courage and to make him cry for mercy. Brébeuf was determined to utter no cry, but to pray to God to forgive them. They put burning sticks about his feet, ran flaming torches up, down, and between his legs, around his neck, and under his armpits. Puzzled that he neither cried out nor winced, they held the firebrands closer till the skin frizzled, then they slashed his flesh with knives.

Brébeuf addressed the captive converts in a strong voice: "My sons, my brothers, let us lift up our eyes to Heaven in our affliction. Let us remember that God is the witness of our sufferings, that very soon He will be our exceedingly great reward. Let us die in our Faith. Let us hope from Him the fulfillment of His promises to us. I have more pity for you than I have for myself. Bear up with courage under the few torments remaining. The sufferings will end with our lives. The grandeur which follows them will never have an end."

A Huron replied: "Echon, our thoughts will be in Heaven while our bodies suffer on earth. Pray to God for us, ask Him to show us mercy, and we shall invoke Him until we die."

His tormenters hacked him with hatchets and knives and stabbed him with javelin heads. "Jesus, have mercy on us!" was the only cry that came from his lips; it was re-echoed by the Christian Hurons.

Incensed by his defiance, the Iroquois cut away his lower lip and thrust a red-hot iron down his throat. As the indomitable priest still held his tall form erect and voiced no sound of pain, no plea for mercy, they tried other means. They brought forth young

Lalemant, that Brébeuf might see them torture him. They had fastened strips of bark, smeared with pitch, about Gabriel's naked body. When the young priest saw the burnt and bleeding body of his superior, aghast and trembling he spoke the words of St. Paul: "We are made a spectacle to the world, to angels and to men."[16] Then he threw himself at Brébeuf's feet, whereupon the savages dragged him away, tied him to a stake, and set fire to the bark fastened about him.

Around Brébeuf's neck the Iroquois hung a collar of six red-hot hatchets that reached over his shoulders; when he stood erect, the irons burned him equally on front and back; if he leaned forward, three irons burned into his back, and if he leaned back, three irons ate into his stomach. "Jesus, have mercy on us!" was his only cry.

Frantic at being unable to break his courage, they attached resinous bark about his thighs and waist and kindled it until he was a living torch.

Among the Iroquois were some renegade Hurons who remembered how Brébeuf had often baptized the sick and dying and consoled them with promises of heavenly reward. And so they hit upon a new torture that was also a mockery. "Echon," said their spokesman, as he poured a kettle of scalding water slowly over his head, "we baptize you that you may be happy in Heaven; for nobody can be saved without a good baptism."

He did not flinch. They cut strips of flesh from his legs and arms and ate them before his eyes.

"You told us," said one of these Hurons, as he stabbed Brébeuf repeatedly with a knife, "that the more one suffers on earth, the happier he is in Heaven. We wish to make you happy; we torment you because we love you, and you ought to thank us for it."

[16] 1 Cor. 4:9.

The priest spoke no word of reproof. He prayed for the forgiveness of his torturers and asked that through his agony the grace of faith might come to them. "Jesus, have mercy!" he cried, lifting his eyes to Heaven.

They cut off his nose, sliced off his upper lip, pulled out his tongue and hacked a piece off it. They placed firebrands against his bleeding flesh and shoved one of them into his mouth. His tall, erect form sagged to the fires about his feet; he was silent now, but his eyes were open, and the Indians gouged them out with a flaming stick.

They dragged Brébeuf from the fire to the torture platform, and there they performed the last rites in honor of Areskoui. They hacked off the charred feet, tore off his scalp, and cut out his heart. This they devoured, and they drank his blood, thinking to imbibe some of his invincible courage. A chief raised his tomahawk over the head of Brébeuf and split the jaw in two. His four hours of torture were finished, at four o'clock in the afternoon.

Brébeuf's wish had been granted, his vow fulfilled. He had given his life for Christ and sanctified with his blood the soil of North America.

Gabriel Lalemant had undergone the preludes of torture. He had been beaten and burned and had suffered vicariously the hours of his companion's torture. The Iroquois thrust pots of corn-meal mush to him and to the Huron captives, bidding them eat plenty so that they would be strong for the evening's sport. Gabriel exhorted his fellow captives to hold fast to the Faith and to die as courageously as their Echon had died.

Toward nightfall his captors hustled him to a torture post. Like Brébeuf, he fell on his knees and kissed it as if it were the Cross of Christ. They beat him with sticks, splintered his hands, and crushed his fingers in their teeth, then bound him loosely to the post. They piled burning sticks at his feet and legs to make him dance, while they sizzled his skin with torches. Again imitating Brébeuf, he uttered the simple cry, "Jesus, have mercy on us!"

The council had decided that Gabriel was to be preserved as a morning sacrifice to Areskoui, and they moderated their tortures during the night so that he would not die outright. After periods of rest, the Iroquois would fasten red-hot axes in his armpits and place glowing tomahawks against his legs. They held burning sticks against his face and neck and forced them into his mouth. Around his waist they fastened a belt of bark, set fire to it, and chortled with glee as the flesh burned.

The renegade Hurons, as they had done with Brébeuf, poured scalding water upon his head, laughing ecstatically as they assured him they were doing this to make certain he would be happy in the next life.

In the still, early hours of morning, before dawn, the Iroquois aroused Gabriel from a spell of resting and resumed their torments. They forced fiery fagots into his mouth, sliced off his tongue, gouged out his eyes, and filled the sockets with glowing coals. They chopped off his hands and pressed hot axes to the stumps of his wrists. His mangled body fell, and they let him lie there while they went off to sleep.

When dawn broke, they found his heart faintly beating. He would be their principal morning sacrifice to Areskoui, for he had proved as brave and unconquerable as Echon. They marveled that one so small and frail could be so lionhearted. During all the long torture, he had made no appeal for pity, no cry of revenge, but only and always the simple "Jesus, have mercy on us!" They could not understand.

Cutting off slices of his flesh, they ate them and supped his blood. They ripped off his scalp and dug out his heart before the tomahawk crashed into his skull. His body they threw on the pile of Huron dead.

From six in the evening, his martyrdom had continued through the ghastly night until nine o'clock in the morning. After fifteen hours of torture rarely, if ever, surpassed in the bloody annals of the Iroquois, the soul of Gabriel Lalemant was freed from its charred and mutilated prison and summoned to join his comrade Jean de Brébeuf in the radiant splendor of God. March 17, 1649 was the date; for Brébeuf it had been the sixteenth.

⟿

The embers around Lalemant's stake had scarcely grown cold when two hundred Iroquois, flushed with their victories, set out through the forest to destroy the mission center of Sainte Marie. If this could be wiped out, they knew, the blow to the reeling, off-balance Hurons would be a deadly one and perhaps final.

Five hundred Hurons, mostly of the Bear clan, were taking up their positions to meet the advancing enemy. Huron scouts came into conflict with the Iroquois, and the skirmish quickly involved the main body of the Hurons. The Iroquois drove them back steadily toward the palisades of Sainte Marie, and here the defenders, notably the Christians of Ossossané, made a desperate stand. Reinforced by a band of Hurons from the new mission of St. Madeleine, they drove the enemy back in confusion to the still-standing palisades of St. Louis. The Iroquois withdrew into the stockade and, after a fierce struggle, were driven out. They sent messengers to the main body of the Iroquois who were at St. Ignace, and the remaining seven hundred of these were soon hurrying to the attack.

One of the wildest battles in Indian history ensued. The Hurons within the palisades of St. Louis numbered only one hundred fifty; many had been killed or disabled by then. But with such desperate abandon did they fight against an enemy vastly superior in number and armed in large part with guns, that they repulsed them again and again. The Hurons held their own far into the night. The principal chief of the Iroquois was severely wounded, and nearly a hundred of his warriors were killed.

At last the overwhelming numbers of the Iroquois prevailed, and when they fought their way into St. Louis, they found but twenty-five Hurons in condition to do battle. Dead and grievously wounded Hurons lay about the splintered palisades, which they had defended with valor unsurpassed in tribal warfare.

Meanwhile, sharp-eyed Huron sentinels at Sainte Marie had discerned shadowy figures stealing from tree to tree and identified them as Iroquois. This was at sunset on the evening of the seventeenth, and the Iroquois scouts were reconnoitering before the renewed attack upon Sainte Marie which impended. The missionaries there kept the lamps burning through the night, and the Huron defenders stayed on the alert. The Jesuit Fathers had not been informed of the fate of Brébeuf and Lalemant, and they were deeply anxious for them as well as for the fate of the entire Huron missionary enterprise. They prayed without ceasing, and St. Joseph, their patron saint, was besieged with invocations. "Those of us who were priests," wrote Ragueneau, "each made a vow to say a Mass in his honor every month for the space of a year; and all the rest bound themselves by vows to diverse penances." The little band were determined to die to a man in the defense of Sainte Marie.

Painfully, March 18 dawned, and the daylight hours slowly passed in tense stillness, as if this were the lull after one tempest and before a second. Father Ragueneau remarked that it was as if "the country were waiting, palsied with fright, some new disaster."

The nineteenth was the feast of St. Joseph, and the tension broke. A group of Hurons arrived at Sainte Marie with the glad news that a panic had seized the Iroquois camp. Fearful that Hurons were approaching them in great numbers to work vengeance, and in spite of the protests of the chiefs, the entire body of the invaders fled in disorder. An elderly squaw, who had escaped from the flames of St. Ignace and who had observed the Iroquois rushing headlong to the south, staggered breathless and exhausted into the large Huron settlement of St. Michel and gave out this news.

Seven hundred Huron braves seized their bows and arrows and rushed forth in pursuit. On the trail they came across the dead bodies of captives tomahawked on the march or tied to trees and burned. The Hurons pressed on for two days, and then they committed the fatuous blunder that was to enable the Iroquois virtually to exterminate the Huron nation and the Jesuit missions among them. Instead of pursuing the enemy with full vigor and perhaps inflicting irreparable disaster upon the exhausted and panicky Iroquois, they gave up the pursuit and returned home. It is uncertain whether their decision was prompted by weariness, by the inability to catch their quarry, or by a wariness of attacking an enemy well armed with muskets. In any case, their move was to prove fatal, for it left intact the Iroquois capacity to demolish the Indian population of Huronia.

On the morning of March 20, the Jesuits at Sainte Marie received full confirmation of the Iroquois retreat. They had heard, too, of the fate of Brébeuf and Lalemant, and the missionary Father Jacques Benin was sent with seven armed Frenchmen to St. Ignace to recover their bodies. The party passed through St. Louis, where the ground was strewn with uncounted dead Hurons and Iroquois. On to St. Ignace they continued, where all was gruesome silence and death. Among the ashes of the burned-out cabins charred corpses were scattered, and they came upon the blackened, mutilated body of Brébeuf. The mangled remains of Lalemant they found with the tortured Hurons a short distance away. Tenderly Father Benin and his companions lifted the two bodies on stretchers of bark and carried them the six miles to Sainte Marie.

They were laid side by side on the floor of the living room. Priests, brothers, *donnés,* and workmen gazed at them with awe and lovingly examined them. Father Bonin knelt for two hours by the body of Gabriel, who had been his dearest friend, and kissed the wounds as he would the relics of a saint. "They are the relics of the love of God which alone triumphs in the death of martyrs," exclaimed Father Ragueneau.

The missionaries had learned, from a few Hurons who had escaped the holocaust at St. Ignace, details of the torture and death of Brébeuf and Lalemant. Confirmation now was before their eyes.

The bodies of Brébeuf and Lalemant were cleansed and clothed in priestly vestments and placed in rough-hewn boxes. Through the night they reposed before the Blessed Sacrament. "We buried these precious relics," relates Father Ragueneau, "on Sunday, March 21, with so much consolation and such tender feelings of devotion in all who were present at the obsequies that I know none who did not desire rather than fear a similar death, and who did not regard himself as blessed to live in a place where, perhaps a few days from then, God would accord him the grace of shedding on a similar occasion both his blood and his life. Not one of us could force himself to pray to God for them, as if they had any need of prayer. On the contrary, our spirits were carried up toward Heaven, where, we had no doubt, their souls resided. Be this as it may, I pray to God that he fulfill in us His will, even to death, as He has done toward them."

Jean de Brébeuf was fifty-six when he gave his body to the Iroquois and his soul to God. With heavy heart Father Ragueneau wrote to his superior in France, telling the loss of their ablest missionary. When Brébeuf first set foot in Huronia twenty-three years before, he recalled, there was not a Christian in that extensive territory. Since that day, nearly seven thousand had been baptized, and to Brébeuf, more than to any other, that long line of conversions must be credited. "Father Jean de Brébeuf," he went on, "had been chosen by God to be the first apostle of the Hurons, the first of our Society to set foot there. Not having found there a single savage who invoked the name of God, he labored there so successfully for the salvation of those poor barbarians that before his death he had the consolation of seeing . . . the Cross of Jesus Christ planted everywhere with glory and adored in a country which from the birth of the world had never been Christian."

Among the papers of Gabriel Lalemant, Father Ragueneau found written the vow he had taken a few years before in France by which he offered himself, body and soul, to the Sacred Heart and begged for the opportunity of shedding his blood for Christ. Father Ragueneau saw that Gabriel's death was the fulfillment of his dedication and the answer to his prayer, that in the Iroquois torture chamber he had won the crown of martyrdom. The smallest and most delicate in health among all the Jesuit missionaries, he had in six months won, by his iron will and unwavering determination, a martyr's end, in companionship with the spiritual and physical giant of the missions, Jean de Brébeuf.

Book Four

≈

Antoine Daniel

≋

Chapter 10

Father Antoine Daniel possessed an unusual talent for making friends quickly and for handling children. Cheerful and light-hearted, "he ravished the hearts of all those who have ever known him," said Paul Ragueneau. Gentle, patient, sociable with old and young, Father Daniel has been known best for his persevering efforts to train the Huron youth in the Christian Faith, that they might plant it among their people, and for his heroic missionary work at the Huron settlement of Teanaustayé.

He was born at the Norman seaport of Dieppe on May 27, 1601. When he had completed his classical studies, he entered a law school, but after a year there, he decided to become a priest. On October 1, 1621, the Jesuit novitiate at Rouen received him. Two years later he pronounced his vows of poverty, chastity, and obedience and was assigned to teach in the College of Rouen.

When he was starting his fourth year of teaching, the college heard exciting news from Canada, where Father Charles Lalemant wrote to his brother Jerome at Rouen: "We are sending you a little Huron boy who is very anxious to visit France and to go to a French school. He has become quite attached to us and, if well

trained, will be of great assistance in converting the Indians."
Amantacha was his name, and he arrived at Rouen amid a flurry of
excitement. His sojourn at the college was in a high degree successful, and it was with an impressive ceremony that he was formally received into the Church. Visitors came from far and near to
be present at the event, and King Louis XIII sent two members
of his Court, the Duc de Longueville and Madame de Villars, to be
sponsors to the new convert. Amantacha was christened, as a
compliment to the monarch, Louis of Holy Faith.

Antoine Daniel was deeply impressed by this whole achievement, and the desire was born in him to labor for the conversion of
the American Indians.

When he had completed four years of teaching, he began his
theology at the College of Clermont. Three years later he was elevated to the priesthood and sent to teach at the college of Eu. He
was burning with the desire to sail to the New World, but the like-
lihood of his doing this grew dim when the English David Kirk
seized Quebec in 1629 and expelled the missionaries.

Father Daniel's brother Charles was the captain of one of the
French vessels that were dispatched to relieve Quebec, but were
scattered by a fog off Newfoundland. When the fog lifted, Captain
Charles Daniel found he was close to Cape Breton Island. He cast
anchor in St. Ann's Bay and learned there that James Stewart, a
Scots lord, had lately founded a colony on the island at Port
Baleines and was seizing all French fishing craft in the surrounding
waters.

Captain Daniel sailed his ship south, demolished Stewart's fort,
and erected a fort of his own at St. Ann's Bay. Leaving there a garrison of forty men, he sailed to France with his English prisoners.
The French flag waved over his colony during the entire three
years that Quebec was held by the English.

The treaty of St. Germain-en-Laye having been signed on March 25, 1632, restoring Canada to France, Captain Daniel set sail for New France in the spring, and at his side stood two young missionaries, Father Davost and Father Antoine Daniel, his brother.

The two priests landed at Cape Breton and began to work among the aborigines of the island. What the place and the people were like is told in a letter written a year later by another missionary, Father Perrault:

At the entrance of the harbor, on the left as you enter, and perched on the top of a bluff is Fort St. Anne, looking toward the northwest. Opposite to it is a small bay. It is a position which competent judges declare is so well chosen that with ten or twelve cannon you could sink every ship that would show itself. Old sailors assure us they have never seen so spacious a port with such facility for landing. Three thousand craft might ride safely at anchor. The harbor forms almost a circle, and is fair to look upon. The tides are moderate and regular, and there is always a depth of thirty or thirty-six feet of water. Although we are in latitude 46 1/2°, the cold is intense, and the winter lasts five or six months of the year. Nevertheless the savages are better off then than in any other place. If they trap fewer beavers in the water, they find more moose on the shore at that time. In summer they live at their ease, on woodchuck, parrot fish, cormorants, and various other sea fowl, and there are otters, mackerel, cod, smelt, and all kinds of fish in season. . . .

The people are not ugly. On the contrary, they are rather good-looking, well built and strong. Their natural hue is white, as you can see from the children, but the heat of the sun and the use of fish oil and elk grease, with which they smear themselves, changes their color as they grow up. They have long black hair but are beardless, so that we are puzzled at times to distinguish the men from the women; though the latter wear more clothes. . . .

Judging from the way they treat us, they are not at all bad. Indeed, there is a certain modesty and gravity in their demeanor which is attractive. They appear to be unwilling to have us know their language, but will listen to us all day and repeat what we say or do. Thus, seeing we pay respect to the cross, they paint it all over their bodies. As far as we can make out, they know nothing about God, or the condition of the soul after death. But perhaps a better acquaintance with their language will change our ideas. Unlike other Indians, they are honest, and although they are polygamists and easily dismiss their wives, there is nothing indecent in their external behavior.

Daniel and Davost labored with meager success among these Indians for a year, then received orders to proceed to Quebec. Davost was detained at Tadoussac, but Daniel went on to Quebec, arriving on June 24, 1633. He was welcomed by the superior, Father Le Jeune, and was handed some letters that contained the first news he had had from home in more than a year.

It was planned that he should travel to Huronia with the Indian flotilla that would be returning there when the Hurons had completed their trading at Quebec, but this was the occasion when the one-eyed chief of the Allumettes, Le Borgne, contrived to influence the natives against the French,[17] and none would make

[17]See chapter 7.

room in their canoes for the mission priests. During the year's delay that was entailed, Daniel and Davost made an intensive study of the Huron tongue; Daniel, in particular, made swift progress.

The following summer the French once more awaited the Hurons. They had heard rumors that the Iroquois were lying in wait to ambush the Hurons, and were apprehensive that the Hurons might not even attempt the journey. Eventually they did appear, but the pestilence that was brooding over Huronia had created an angry mood in them. Cajoled by numerous presents, they cheerlessly took on the three missionaries who were to make the trip and set out on July 7, 1634.

This classic land-and-water journey to Huronia — beset by a burning sun, dreary silences, exhausting portages, miserable food, swarms of mosquitoes, endless paddling — was hardship enough for Daniel in his maiden voyage, particularly with the Indians in such a surly state, but the nightmare was capped when they ejected him from his canoe onto the Island of the Allumettes and continued without him. He might have perished in this wild country had he not been rescued by a traveling Bear chief who took him into his canoe. He arrived, worn out, at the Bear village of Quieuindohan, which the French called La Rochelle, and from there he made his way to Toanché.

Here, with the other Jesuits, he embarked upon his missionary sojourn. He visited the sick in their cabins, brought little delicacies to them, and instructed as many as he could in the fundamentals of the Faith.

The following year found him among the Algonquins toward the south, where we see him kneeling at midnight by the side of an Iroquois captive who was staked to the ground. While his captors were shaking firebrands over the captive, causing sparks to shower down on his naked, mangled body, Antoine Daniel spoke words of

Christian assurance to him, instructed him briefly, and prepared him for Baptism, which he administered before the Iroquois died the next day.

Later Daniel was at Ihonatiria, where one day a number of wounded Hurons rushed in. Their band had been set upon by Iroquois, who tomahawked some and took others prisoner. Among those who escaped was young Amantacha, he who had been baptized Louis at the College of Rouen when Daniel was teaching there. Louis, it developed, had wavered in his Christian practices when he returned to Huronia and had caused the missionaries deep concern. Now this massacre from which he narrowly escaped brought a decided change in his life, for he was convinced he owed his life to God's protection. Soon he brought his whole family into the Faith, except his father, and he did not again lapse; he became a lay apostle and an untiring teacher of the Christian truths.

Later on, Louis Amantacha and his father joined Father Daniel in an expedition to Quebec. The father, a shiftless braggart and a moocher, had by then been persuaded to give thoughtful consideration to accepting the Faith, and during the long trip to Quebec his son counseled him in this manner: "Father, when you embrace Christianity, do not do so for anything you hope to get out of it. When you are among the French, refrain from going around the cabins to have a good time. Don't be regarded as a beggar. Try to see Monsieur de Champlain, and keep near the Fathers."

Father Daniel's special work during his stay at Ihonatiria was with the children. Their parents had not trained or disciplined them, and they were utterly lawless and bad-tempered, but with infinite forbearance and kindliness the missionary became a favorite with them and made striking headway in acquainting them with the elements of Christianity. Having taught them to sing, he proceeded to train the children to chant the Our Father, the Hail

Mary, and the Commandments, which he had rendered into Huron rhymes. Formed into a choir, they added beauty and solemnity to the chapel services and attracted great numbers of their elders to Mass. The children did not restrict their singing to the chapel. They chanted and sang in their own cabins, and many Indian adults learned from their children Christian truths that they refused to hear from the missionaries.

Daniel's success with the young Indians was so marked that when the Jesuit superior in Quebec decided to establish a school for Huron boys there, Daniel was selected as its director. His Jesuit confreres in Huronia were loath to lose him, for he handled the language with facility and was loved by them for his cheerful companionship, his unfailing friendliness, and his good humor.

It was 1636, and his departure with the trading flotilla was scheduled for July 22. Since a school for Huron boys could scarcely function without Huron boys present, Daniel appealed to the people to allow some of their young ones to journey with him to Quebec. The Faith was not yet strong in the hearts of these Hurons, and the religious motive for sending their sons was not stressed; rather, Daniel explained that to send their boys to the school would more strongly cement their friendship with the French and would enable them to become excellent traders. His words seemed persuasive, and a dozen families agreed, so providing a sizable nucleus.

The canoes were loaded with furs and provisions, and twelve Huron boys bade tearful and reluctant farewells to their families. They were straggling down to the canoes, when the wailings of their mothers became too much for them. All but three turned about and fled to the consolation of their mothers' arms. No amount of pleading could release them, so Father Daniel contented himself with the remaining three hopefuls.

Twenty-four days later an Indian beached his canoe at Three Rivers and handed a letter to Father Le Jeune. It was from Father Daniel and it said:

> I am held here at the Island of the Allumettes. The Indians will not let us pass, because Chief Le Borgne is dead, and his relatives have not been covered. You know what that means. Their grief has not been assuaged by rich presents. We cannot satisfy them, and although they are willing to let the French go down the river, they are detaining the Hurons, but I told them I would not go without my Indians.
>
> I saw Fathers Garnier and Chastellain about three days' journey up from here. They seemed to be having a good time, for they had their shoes on and were not paddling. I was so delighted that I gave the savages some of the weed which we detest and which they adore — tobacco. It costs a good deal here this year, but I would give ten times as much to get out of this scrape at the Island. It is of the greatest importance that I should do so. Unfortunately, however, although I promised you twelve pupils, I have only three, but one of them is the son of a great chief. I have also some older people with me whom you will see. Would you please tell M. du Plessis that although I have only a few canoes I have a good supply of provisions?

The letter ends, "Signed under the glare of a piece of burning bark, which is the only candle we have in this country."

The main body of Father Daniel's party, with himself in the lead of the flotilla and Davost bringing up the rear, arrived at Three Rivers on August 19. "When we saw Father Daniel," relates Le Jeune, "our hearts began to melt. His face was wreathed in smiles, but he was all spent. He was in his bare feet; he held a paddle in his hand, wore a ragged soutane, and his breviary was slung by a string around his neck. His shirt was rotting on his back. He saluted all the chiefs and Frenchmen, and then we embraced. After adoring the Blessed Sacrament, we all withdrew to my little room, where he told us how the Faith was progressing among the Hurons. Then he gave me his papers and the account of the mission."

After the Hurons had done with their trading and had held the usual powwows, they were ready to depart. And of the three boys who were to enter the new school, only one, Satouta of the Bear clan, was willing to remain; the other two wished to go home. Daniel and Le Jeune pleaded with the Indians to keep their word. Even the general of the fleet, who was there, lent a hand. He convened a council with the Hurons and said to them, "Why do you not show the friendship you profess for the French? You give beaver robes to the French, and the French give you hatchets; this is not an evidence of real love. We show love by sending the Blackrobes to live with you and to teach you. Not one of you will live among the French. Why do you not trust us? Why is there only one village of Hurons that shows its love for the French?"

An old chief supported the general's plea. He declared it was a shame that only the Bears should show any confidence in the French. Turning to his nephew Joseph Tewatiron, he said, "You will remain here; have no fear; the French will treat you well."

Not to be outdone, the father of Satouta, the Bear, made a little speech: "My son," he exhorted, "be firm; do not change your mind. You are going among good people. Do not take anything without Father Antoine's leave. Obey the Blackrobes. Keep away from the Montagnais. Don't go into a canoe with the French, for you might misunderstand each other and quarrel. If you kill a deer, keep the skin and give away the flesh. Stay here until next year, and we shall see what is to be done."

And so there were two little scholars for the Huron school. When the speechmaking was done, Le Jeune and Daniel took their two charges to the general's vessel. As they were leaving, the elders of the boys continued to urge them to keep up their courage and not to steal anything, as that was contrary to the custom of the French. The vessel hoisted anchor, swung around for Quebec, and cut the waters of the St. Lawrence to the booming of all the cannons on the fort.

"And there," remarked Le Jeune, "you have your seminary; all I need now is a place to put it and the means to support it. The trouble is that these little savages come to you as naked as your hand; for when you dress them up French style, the parents take away all their old clothes and expect plentiful presents for having given you their prodigies."

A third Huron boy joined the group, and the French trader and interpreter Nicolet recruited two more. So Father Daniel's enrollment totaled five little copper-skinned youngsters. They were lodged temporarily in the Fathers' Quebec residence. To provide funds for their education and care, five of the French workmen had to be discharged.

They erected a school on the bank of the St. Charles River, two miles from Quebec, and they named it Notre Dame des Anges (Our Lady of the Angels) after the Jesuit residence; for both were dedicated to the Blessed Virgin.

That the pupils were far from being angels soon became abundantly clear. Unaccustomed to discipline of any kind, they were, in the words of the *Relation*, "as hard to manage as wild asses." That the young educator, Father Daniel, had no easy time of it is suggested in the account written by Le Jeune: "If crosses and trials are the most solid foundations of the edifice which is to raise its pinnacles to Heaven, then the school for the Hurons is well established. Its birth is full of labor, its first steps full of sadness; I pray God that its end may be accompanied by joy and peace."

Patience, good nature, and determination won the day. The pupils were taught to read and write; they learned their prayers, the chief doctrines of the Christian Faith, and the manner of serving Mass. They were trained in carpentry, woodcarving, and drawing, and they had practice in oratory, esteemed by the natives as the greatest of the arts.

But the school had not been long under way when the first of a series of misfortunes struck it. The two most promising pupils, Tsiko and Satouta, became seriously ill. The Fathers did what they could for them, but their condition worsened rapidly. They were baptized, Tsiko died, and then little Satouta. "Behold," wrote Le Jeune, "the two eyes of our school extinguished within a brief period, the two columns overthrown!" It was not yet September, and the enrollment was down to three.

While the boys had been ill, Father Daniel had been a father and a mother to them, nursing their sickness, staying at their side through night and day, forgetful of food and rest for himself. The strain was too much, and when the second boy died, Daniel collapsed. In his run-down condition, he had contracted influenza; he tossed about in a fever, which was aggravated by worry over the repercussions the deaths might have upon the natives in Huronia. Every assurance had been given the Indians that the boys would be well cared for and that they would be safely returned. Would the Hurons, in their superstition and egged on by the conniving sorcerers, think the Blackrobes had caused the death of their children?

As it developed, however, a plague was devastating Huronia, and the loss of the two children was held to be merely a part of the general calamity.

One of the three surviving pupils became homesick and found it difficult to adjust himself to the school's regulations. Daniel dismissed him, and that left two, Armand and Joseph. Five recruits came the next summer, but most of these showed little interest in knowledge or in discipline. Reports the *Relation:* "They gave themselves up, according to their custom, to thieving, gormandizing, gaming, idleness, lying, and similar irregularities." One ran away, another showed himself so corrupt he had to be dismissed; the last three of the recruits stole a canoe, loaded it with plunder, and vanished in the dawn over the waters of the St. Lawrence. Again there were two, Armand and Joseph.

But Father Daniel persevered. The progress made by these two, and the fervor of their faith, repaid him for the discouragements he had suffered. Later on, he was certain, their apostolate among their own people would justify the expenditure of so much time and effort.

Alarming rumors concerning the safety of the Huron missions were afloat. For a year the plague had been ravaging the country there, and the missionaries were blamed for this. A general massacre of the French at any moment was expected, and Governor Montmagny, although he had a slim garrison, considered sending a band of soldiers to the aid of his countrymen.

But another plan was suggested, and this prevailed: Armand and Joseph would be sent to Huronia and prove by their own safety and progress that the Blackrobes designed no evil. Father Daniel would accompany them to add his testimony and to warn the Hurons that soldiers would be sent to punish any who harmed the French.

Armand and Joseph readily acquiesced in the project; they and Daniel would be accompanied by a Frenchman and a party of Algonquins.

Raging spring floods had swollen the river, and the danger from this condition was added to the constant menace of footloose Iroquois. As Armand's canoe was rounding a point, it ran into a froth of rapids and was upset with its two occupants; the other, an Algonquin, swam to shore, but Armand had been entrusted with a box containing a chalice and other Mass utensils. As he struggled in the swirling waters to retrieve this, the treacherous current pulled him under, and for a few moments he seemed to be lost. His faith was with him, and he prayed: "O Master of Life, Thou canst do all things. Thou canst let me die or make me live. Thou art my God." He fought his way to the surface and to a rock protruding above. He was rescued from this, bruised and exhausted. He lamented that he had not saved the precious box, and he reproached himself bitterly.

"It is enough," said Father Antoine, "that you have been saved. Let us thank God for that."

A few days later the canoes became separated, and Father Daniel was the last to arrive at a long and difficult portage. Famished, enfeebled by the long illness he had endured at Quebec, and worn out by the arduous journey over rocks and through swamps and woodland undergrowth, he reeled under the pack he was shouldering and fell to the ground in a faint. When he returned to consciousness, he was too weak to rise. A few gooseberries were within his reach, and these became the first food he had had that day. He got up on his feet, and his legs collapsed under him.

It was the law of the wilderness that to drop from weariness on a journey was to be abandoned by the Indians. All missionaries had been warned years before, and ever since, that if one were accidentally hurt on the way to Huronia, or if one fell sick, no help must be expected from the natives.

"I thought of Agar and the prophet Elias in the wilderness," wrote Daniel, "and I wondered if God would help me as He did them, but my sins prevented me from hoping for such a favor. However, I was consoled by the thought that if I died, it was through obedience. I remained an hour or two in this state when my men, perceiving my absence, came back to look for me. I asked them for something to eat, but they said they had nothing. They helped me up, took my pack, and encouraged me to walk, and soon we came to a rivulet which refreshed me somewhat and gave me strength to reach Allumettes toward evening. There I found my two seminarists, and also the young Frenchman, who were very much alarmed, for they had been waiting for me for two days. I met Armand's relatives and went to their cabin, but at night the Algonquins came and asked me to go with them to sing their litanies. I was very tired, but I dragged myself to their wigwam, for it was sweeter for me than for them. We heard that the Fathers were safe, though they had been in considerable danger, and so after remaining a week on the Island to recuperate, we resumed our journey and reached Ihonatiria on July 9, having left Montreal on June 11."

It is a rare individual who, in the last stages of physical exhaustion, is ready to surrender the rest that nature demands and stagger to an Indian wigwam and listen to its unsubtle inhabitants sing litanies that were "sweeter for me than for them. "

During the relatively short sojourn with these Algonquins, Daniel accomplished wonders, under adverse conditions, in teaching the words and melodies of Christian litanies in their own tongue — and making them delight in it. The *Relation* tells how, when the party paddled by an Algonquin settlement, the people would chant these litanies at the top of their voices. Natives who could not be persuaded by any inducement to say prayers, Daniel discovered, would sing these same prayers with gusto if set to rhyme and music. None of the other Jesuit missionaries could match Daniel's success in this department.

When Father Antoine reached Ihonatiria at last, gaunt, emaciated, more ghost than man, he was relieved to learn that his confreres were alive and free and that the storm of resentment against their imagined mischief had subsided.

Armand fulfilled all expectations, and more. He amazed the Jesuits with his fearless championship of the Faith. Contrary to Indian tradition, he did not hesitate to take a strong position against even the most powerful chiefs in defense of Christianity and the missionaries. Like one of them, he moved among his people, explained the tenets of the Christian Faith and urged them to keep the Commandments. His example was even more eloquent than his words. He led a life of prayer and moral perfection that astounded the Indians. Still in the first years of youth, he became one of the bravest of their warriors, and he appeared to enjoy immunity against the enemy's weapons. "God protects me," he would say. "The arrows seem to come straight at me in a shower, and then in a most remarkable manner they turn aside."

In the summer of 1642, Armand was the key figure in an astonishing affair. He was the only Christian in a boatful of braves belonging to St. Michel, one of Daniel's missions, who were returning from the warpath. They were crossing Lake Simcoe when a violent storm overcame them. Their little boat was tossed by mountainous waves and would, it seemed, be overwhelmed at any moment. The Indians were singing the death chant.

Armand cried out to them these words: "Comrades, your voices are drowned in this storm. They can never penetrate into Hell, where your miserable demons are burning. You call on them in vain. They cannot hear you. For me, I shall have recourse to God, for I know that He is everywhere and will surely hear my prayers and, if He wishes, will have pity on us, although you have offended Him." Addressing the man in the stern, he said, "Stop. Let the canoe go with the wind, so that the one in front will not have to fend off the waves that are dashing against us. He must be at rest to pray." Humbly they all bent their heads, while Armand prayed aloud to God as his devotion prompted. Suddenly the waters about them became as calm and smooth as glass, while elsewhere the storm continued with frantic tumult. The waves, says the *Relation*, were "great enough to sink a thousand canoes had they been there."

When they returned home safely, the Hurons reported this occurrence to Father Daniel and to all in the settlement. The news not long after had spread throughout Huronia.

Armand distinguished himself for bravery in the many clashes of Huron and Iroquois along the St. Lawrence, and many of the *Relations* record his feats. At the same time, he was a leader in the sodality of the Servants of Mary, which sent birch-bark letters and wampum belts to the great shrines of Europe. The members of this sodality met at daybreak on Sundays and feast days to recite the Rosary. An exhortation, sometimes by the Jesuit director and at other times by one of the Indian prefects, preceded each decade. At the Mass that followed, they sang the *Gloria in Excelsis* and the *Credo* in Huron. On the evenings of these days, they assembled for Benediction and sang the litanies or a hymn to the Blessed Virgin. The members of the sodality were convincing evidence to the missionaries that the life of piety and high morality were possible in those pagan circumstances.

Armand heard two Masses every day, kneeling on the bare ground. The bitterest cold did not deter him. He recited the Rosary five or six times daily and inspired his wife, Félicité, to similar practices.

Years later, the *Relation* for 1655 described the abject condition of the Hurons who had taken refuge at the Isle d'Orléans after the

Iroquois had destroyed the missions and scattered those Indians. In the course of the recital, the narrative says, "This year there died at this place a remarkable young Indian who for seventeen years not only never proved false to the promises of his Baptism, but who, on the contrary, improved each year in piety and devotion. His name is Armand Andewarahan." Father Daniel's pupil was steadfast to the end, and he left behind him a memory of heroism and holiness.

It was not long after Father Antoine Daniel's return to Huronia that Jerome Lalemant arrived as the new superior. In assigning the missionaries to their several areas of duty, he sent Daniel, along with five other Jesuit Fathers, to Ossossané, on Nottawasaga Bay. With its 2,500 inhabitants, this was one of the most populous villages in the district. Daniel spent a year there, then was assigned with Father Le Moyne to Cahiagué,[18] near Lake Simcoe. This village was dedicated to St. John the Baptist. They were warmly welcomed by the friendly Hurons when they arrived on November 1, 1639. Cahiagué was the largest village of the Arendaronon clan, and the people recalled pridefully how Champlain, when he visited Huronia in 1615, had stayed longer there than in any other village.

The memory of Champlain was deeply imbedded in these Indians, because of his kindness and his unprepossessing manner of authority; among all the missionaries, he was highly honored, too, because of the irreproachable goodness of his life. "Would to God," say the *Relations*, "that all the Frenchmen who came out here in the beginning had been like him. We would not now be obliged to blush when the savages cast up to us the shameless debauchery of the *voyageurs*, and ask why they should believe in

[18]Near the present town of Hawkstone.

Hell, since many of the Frenchmen whom they saw seemed to have no fear of it."

When Daniel and his companions had been welcomed to Cahiagué, every cabin strove for the privilege of lodging them. The Jesuits were feasted, honored with many speeches, and burdened with presents. The esteem they enjoyed was heightened when the smallpox came down upon the village. The priests had little rest as they went from cabin to cabin, doing what they could to assuage the sickness. The Indians' gratitude was immeasurable, and the missionaries looked to a handsome harvest of converts.

Overnight the mood reversed itself. The change was as dismaying as it had been sudden. The fickle natives were as sensitive to every new whim of witchcraft, sorcery, or dream compulsion as the weathervane to the breeze. A hunter, who had been absent from the village when the missionaries came, arrived one day in a state of excitement.

"When I was alone in the forest," he reported, "a beautiful young man appeared to me and declared that he was the Lord of the World: 'I am the one whom the French call Jesus, but they do not know me. I have pity on your nation and take it under my protection, and therefore I want to tell you the reason of the sickness that is destroying you all, and what you are to do to stop it. The cause of it is the presence of those strangers. You see them going everywhere, two and two, in their black gowns. That is to spread the pestilence. The only thing to do is to drive them out. For those who are already attacked by the disease, tell your sachems to get a certain kind of water and let them carry it to the sick all night long, while the braves go from cabin to cabin as madmen. This must be kept up until daybreak. Go as fast as you can, and have all this done."

This order threw the settlement into an uproar. Three successive councils discussed it, and at last it was decided that the ceremonies prescribed must be carried out to the letter. In a matter of hours, the village resounded with the shouts of chiefs exhorting the braves to carry on like madmen. Hysteria seized both men and women. Decked out in hideous masks and grotesque attire, braves danced through the streets, screamed threats, and looted cabins. Others, stark naked, yelled and danced themselves into frenzy. "Meanwhile," the *Relation* says, "six old men were trotting around in solemn silence carrying the huge caldrons of water prescribed by the apparition, and like so many apothecaries pouring it down the throats of the sick."

The missionaries, who still had not been driven out as it had been directed they should be, were lodging with the chief. The ritual was begun there each day, and they could not escape seeing the riotous and disillusioning display of satanic madness. To emancipate the Indians forevermore from superstition, they perceived, could be accomplished only with time, Herculean labor, and abundant grace.

During the days of pandemonium, the priests, except Chaumonot, were unharmed. A young brave was battering this missionary's head with a rock and would have killed him if Daniel and some Hurons had not intervened.

The madness ran its course, and all was relatively quiet again. But it was plain to see that the Hurons were suspicious and hostile toward the missionaries, and what this might lead to, nobody could tell. But if the Jesuits were to win any appreciable number of Indians to Christianity, if, indeed, they were even to survive, they knew they must uproot any cause for antagonism. With this in mind, Daniel prevailed upon his friend Atironta, an important village chief, to summon a council of the leaders. When the council was convened, Daniel appeared before them and reasoned with them in these words:

I am here to refute the lies that have been spread about us. It has been said that the missionaries are the cause of the plague. Then how do you account for the fact that the epidemic had started long before we came?

And if our object had been to kill you, would we have nursed the sick? Would we have prepared special food for them? Would we have given up our sleep and rest to snatch the dying from the hands of death? Would we have prayed for their recovery? Would we have blessed them with holy water to bring about their cure? Are there not men, women, and children in this village who would now be lying cold and stiff in the winter snows awaiting burial if it had not been for our care?

Daniel's brave speech blunted the edge of the chiefs' antagonism, and it was not long before the missionaries were entering the cabins again, caring for the sick and instructing all who cared to listen. By spring they had baptized about one hundred forty, and some of these converts were manifesting a genuine fidelity to the Christian Faith that seemed to promise better days ahead.

In 1641 the missions of St. John the Baptist at Cahiagué and St. Joseph at Teanaustayé were combined into one, under the care of Daniel and Le Moyne. Teanaustayé, a populous village of more than sixteen hundred and about twelve miles southeast of the central mission of Sainte Marie, had many converts resulting from missionary labors of the years before, and there Father Daniel was destined to stay for seven years more.

The Christian colony was exemplary and provided Daniel and Le Moyne with a large and solid nucleus from the outset. Sunday was a great festival day, and many received Communion, having prepared for it days before. At midday on Sundays and holy days, the village bell summoned Christians to the Rosary, a sermon, and Benediction, and there were impressively long processions through the village, ending at the Christians' own cemetery, which they kept separate from the common burial ground. They built a large chapel in 1646, with a bell and beautiful Indian decorations.

During these years the Iroquois posed a perpetual menace, and to this the village of Teanaustayé was especially sensitive, since it lay the nearest of all the villages to the route followed by Iroquoian war parties. Sneak raids were common, and against them the Hurons kept always on the alert; in one raid, a number of squaws who had gone to till the fields were carried away; in another, some Huron sentries, ascertained to be sleeping, were tomahawked.

At this exposed outpost, Father Daniel patiently, brightly, always with fine grace, advanced the Christian cause. Instruction was constant, baptisms frequent. The exasperating distractions that were of the very essence of missionary labor caused him no slackening in the rigorous performance of the spiritual exercises; indeed, it appears from his notes that the fervor of his spiritual life developed with the years. He would spend long hours in prayer, extending his devotions far into the night, when the Indians were stretched out in slumber on all sides of him. He knew, in regard to the Iroquois, that he walked always on the thin crust of a volcano whose occasional tremors warned that it might erupt shatteringly at any moment. Yet his letters to France were unvaryingly cheerful, and of the danger of sudden death they gave no hint. All seemed to be advancing serenely in the cause of Christ.

Annually, Daniel repaired to Sainte Marie for the retreat that brought missionaries from scattered posts of duty every summer. It was deeply refreshing for these Ignatian soldiers of Christ to see one another after months of anxiety, primitive living, and frequently discouraging labors in their lonely places. But they had not come together merely for social exchange; they had come for spiritual renewal, and for eight days they would observe silence, meditate, pray, and listen to spiritual conferences. Their common and individual goal was closer union with God. They must fashion their interior selves into the likeness of Christ, so that their actions, no less than their words, would mirror and partake of the character of their Master. In no other way could they persuasively introduce Him to the people of the wilderness.

When these retreats were ended, a mood of joyous gaiety would bubble up among the little band, as always after prolonged spiritual exercises. And so it was on July 2, 1648. There would be relaxation now; there would be merry companionship, reminiscing over schooldays in France, exchanging mission experiences. As they were chatting that day, Antoine Daniel rose to leave. They begged him to take at least a day's rest, for it would be a year before they all would meet again. But Antoine, although surely the most sociable of them all, and relishing their cheery affability, was concerned for his flock and for the dangers that were constantly around them. He bade his confreres an affectionate adieu and was on his way. As always, his Huron friends gave him a warm welcome, for his place in their hearts was secure.

On the next day, the third, he heard confessions, urging all his friends to be prepared at every moment for disaster. "Remember," he said, "you know not the day nor the hour."

At daybreak the following morning, July 4, he celebrated Mass. When he had finished, he turned to speak to his flock. The sudden cry "The Iroquois! The Iroquois are here!" interrupted his discourse and curdled the blood of all who were there. The braves hurried to seize their weapons; the women and children fled into the woods. Father Antoine urged the warriors to defend themselves and their families with the utmost valor, then hurried to the cabins in which the aged and the sick were unable to rise from their mats. He baptized and consoled many, and said to them, "Brothers, today we shall be in Heaven."

The Iroquois were assaulting the palisades in strength, and the Hurons fought them off with desperation. But it was plain that it was only a matter of time before the much superior numbers of the attackers would prevail, and the Hurons, seeing all hope of ultimate safety crumbling, flocked to their spiritual leader, whom the unbaptized implored for the sacrament. Father Daniel dipped his handkerchief in water and baptized them by sprinkling.

The church seemed to many the best place to die, and into it they crowded. Seeing this, Daniel hurried to it and urged the people to escape while there was yet time. I shall remain here," he said, "while there is a soul to save. My life is of no account if I can help you."

The Iroquois had broken through the palisades. They poured through the streets and with upraised tomahawks into the cabins. Soon they were streaming toward the chapel. Daniel advanced toward them and forbade them to enter. For a moment they paused in amazement at such a spectacle; then they rained a shower of arrows upon him, and a bullet pierced his heart. With the name of Jesus on his lips, he fell to the ground. The Iroquois pounced on him, tore off his garments, hacked his body, and perpetrated every manner of indignity upon it.

By now the flames from the cabins which the Iroquois had fired were licking at the church. Soon it was a blazing furnace, and into the fiercest part of the fire they tossed the body of Father Daniel; this was near the altar, upon which he had so short a time before offered up the Holy Sacrifice, and there the holocaust was completed. His body was so thoroughly consumed that not a vestige of his bones was ever found.

Saints of the American Wilderness

The Iroquois followed through to the end of their enterprise with methodical butchery. Having set the village afire and having killed uncounted Hurons there, they pursued the women and children into the woods. The cries of the babies betrayed the hiding places of their mothers; some were butchered on the spot, mothers and children together; others were led away captive. How many Hurons were killed that ghastly day is not known, but about seven hundred prisoners, mostly women and children, were taken by the Iroquois when they turned their backs that night upon the charred and gutted ruins of Teanaustayé and the mission church of St. Joseph. Those who escaped found refuge at Sainte Marie.

With the martyrdom of Father Antoine Daniel, the Hurons lost a devoted friend, counselor, and priest; his fellow missionaries lost a comrade of singular charm and engaging friendliness. Grief was spread wide throughout Huronia, and Bancroft says that "the Huron nation were his mourners."

Father Paul Ragueneau said, in writing to the Father General in Rome about the destruction of St. Joseph's mission:

> In charge of this church was Father Antoine Daniel, a man of great courage and endurance, whose gentle kindness was conspicuous among his great virtues. . . . Antoine had just finished his fourteenth year at the Huron mission, everywhere a useful man, and assuredly raised up for the salvation of those tribes. . . . Yet the divine goodness toward him seems to have been remarkable, for he had finished, only the first day of July, eight days of continuous spiritual exercises of the Society in this house of Sainte Marie; and on the very next day, without any delay, or even one day's rest, he hastened to his own mission. Verily, he burned with a zeal for God more intense than any flame that consumed his body.

Book Five

∽

Charles Garnier
Noël Chabanel

~

Chapter 11

Father Charles Garnier, the Apostle to the Hurons and the Petuns, has left a memory of exceptional heroism. In the last moments of the agony that ended in his death, he tried with his waning energies to save the soul of another.

He was born in Paris, but sources do not agree as to whether this was on May 25, 1605, or May 26, 1606. His grandfather had been commandant of the little town of Pithiviers and was hanged by the Prince de Condé for refusing to abjure his Catholic Faith when the town surrendered. When this man's son, Charles's father, became secretary to the council of Henry III and treasurer of Normandy, he petitioned the monarch to remove from the commandant's name the taint that accompanied it by reason of a death which in the military category was a disgrace, although in the religious category it was martyrdom. The king acquiesced, issuing a proclamation that affirmed the heroic death of the commandant and declared it to be a national glory. A magnificent mausoleum was erected in the Carmelite church at Pithiviers, where he was entombed, and on the tomb were recorded his brave defense of the town and other deeds of valor.

Charles Garnier received his early schooling at Louis-le-Grand, where he led his fellow scions of the nobility in studies. He was a member of a group whom other students called the *beati* ("happy" or "blessed"), whether because of their happy disposition or exceptional piety, we do not know. There was evidence even then of a strongly religious spirit in Garnier. Much of the money he received from home went to a prisoners' relief society, and some was used to buy up indecent books, which he promptly burned. On one occasion, he was returning with some companions from a game of handball; in the Faubourg St. Denis his companions stopped in at a tavern, The Wealthy Plowman, patronized by the well-to-do. Charles refused to enter, and he waited outside for the others as a servant would wait for his master. "Such beginnings," remarks Father Ragueneau, "spoke of a distinguished sanctity in time to come."

On September 5, 1624, Charles entered the Jesuit novitiate in Paris. It was a step to which he had long been looking forward with zest, although it meant a great sacrifice on the part of his father, who was devoted to him. "If I did not love your Society [of Jesus] above all others," his father said to the Jesuit superior, "I would not give you a child who, from the time of his birth to the present, has never been guilty of one act of disobedience or caused me the least displeasure."

In the novitiate were three students who were greatly to stimulate Charles's yearning for the foreign missions: Francis Le Mercier, René Menard, and Peter Chastellain. Le Mercier was destined to spend fifteen years in the Huron missions and narrowly miss martyrdom on several occasions; his name is alongside Garnier's in the "death letter" that Brébeuf wrote at Ossossané. Menard would be Charles's companion at Teanaustayé; he spent twenty years in Quebec and nine in Huronia and penetrated farther west than any missionary had yet gone. He ultimately met his death, abandoned and alone, while searching for a band of Huron Christians in the wilderness that is now Wisconsin. Chastellain was to be Charles Garnier's closest friend in the Jesuit order and was to spend fourteen years among the Hurons. Charles once wrote his brother Henry, a Carmelite monk, "You will always have an intention in your prayers for Father Chastellain if you don't forget me, because he and I are one."

Charles Garnier was never strong, and his noble birth and upbringing had accustomed him to a life of refinement that he knew would not be his among the far-off missions upon which his thoughts increasingly converged. "Garnier's face was beardless," writes Francis Parkman, "although he was above thirty years old. For this he was laughed at by his friends in Paris, but admired by the Indians, who thought him handsome. His constitution, bodily or mental, was by no means robust. From boyhood, he had shown a delicate and sensitive nature, a tender conscience, and a proneness to religious emotion. . . . With none of the bone and sinew of rugged manhood, he entered, not only without hesitation, but with eagerness, on a life which would have tried the boldest; and, sustained by the spirit within him, he was more than equal to it."

Garnier completed his philosophical studies at Clermont, taught for three years at Eu, and returned to Clermont for his theology. It was at this period that his eldest brother, Joseph, created some anxiety among the Garnier father and sons. This brother, occupying a prominent place in the world, had fallen into a life of dissipation and showed clear indications of losing his faith. Charles's letters to Carmelite Henry show his concern. In October 1631 he wrote, "I saw him at Argenteuil on the ninth of this month on my way to Paris. I found him much better than when I left home but not what I wanted. I have prayed so much for him that, if my prayers were agreeable to God, I cannot understand how he remains in the state in which he is."

Charles's prayers were not without fruit, for a striking change occurred in Joseph. Having astonished his family once by declaring that if he ever had to choose between living in a Capuchin convent and Hell, He would prefer Hell, now to the greater astonishment of all, he presented himself to the Capuchins and asked to be admitted. Knowing something of his reputation, they demurred, whereupon he informed them that he would remain on the doorstep a beggar until they let him in. In the face of his persistence they yielded. Now the Garniers had a Carmelite, a Jesuit, and a Capuchin in the family.

Later on, even Henry the Carmelite was to cause uneasiness to Charles, for he came increasingly to accuse himself of melancholy, bodily ailments, and unwillingness to accept the burdens placed on him. Possibly the monk was piously exaggerating his spiritual troubles and Charles was accepting his complaints too literally. In any case, Charles peppered him with hortatory letters for years, even from the wigwams of the Hurons. "I am sorry," he says, "to hear of the many cares that beset you. If you find anyone who is wise and holy and has at the same time a special liking for you, I would advise you to open your heart to him. I think you have a right to go to him as often as your rules and superiors will allow. You need someone like that, and it has to be someone who knows you well and knows all the circumstances. I don't think you can dispense with such a friend." It might be that Charles spoke as much from experience as from innate wisdom, for he himself had found in his friend Chastellain a confidant of rare prudence and sound judgment.

Shortly after his ordination in 1635, Charles made known his earnest wish to be assigned to the Indian missions, and it is little wonder that his father, who had given three sons to religion, stormed in rebellious protest, arguing that he had already made more than a reasonable contribution to the Church. Charles's superiors, deferring to his father's opposition, and being more than glad to keep with them a young priest whom they esteemed highly, denied his request for almost a year.

Charles prayed unceasingly and renewed from time to time his request for permission to cross the Atlantic to New France. At last his father desisted from overt opposition, the Jesuits consented, and Charles started on foot for Dieppe, delirious with joy. He did not wait for a companion, and he had taken no provisions. It was winter, the roads were vile, and several times he fell in a faint from exhaustion. He reached Dieppe and there boarded the *St. Joseph,* which sailed on April 8, 1636, under the command of the new governor of Canada, Charles de Montmagny. The beloved Father Chastellain and two other missionaries also were on the vessel.

Garnier did not wait until he reached New France to redeem souls. During the voyage, he won back a number of fallen-away French Catholics, including a member of the crew who had led a dissipated life and had not been to the sacraments for ten years. Conditions on board were conducive to religious endeavor, for Montmagny instituted a regime that might have done justice to a religious community. "Of course," wrote Garnier to his father from Quebec, "there was many a hardship. . . . I missed Mass only twelve or thirteen times during the voyage, which lasted two months. Our chapel was in the cabin of Monsieur le General [Bouchard]. One part of the crew assisted at the first Mass, the rest at the second. At the Elevation there were two fusillades of musketry, and on Sundays and feast days two salvos of artillery. Our 'parishioners' went to Communion, and M. de Montmagny set them the example, besides delighting everyone with the care he took of a poor family on board who were all sick. Orders were posted up on the ship prohibiting profanity, stealing, and quarreling. Everything, indeed, was so religiously conducted that even the blessed bread was distributed on Sundays, as if the travelers had been at home in their own parish church. In the afternoon there was a sermon, with vespers and compline. On weekdays, besides daily prayers, catechism was taught to the children, and after supper a half hour's reading from *The Lives of the Saints*, usually in the general's cabin but sometimes on deck for the sailors."

The ship reached Quebec on June 11, 1636, and Governor Montmagny led a procession to church, where a solemn *Te Deum* was sung in thanksgiving for a safe voyage. On their way to the church, they had passed a wayside cross. "Behold," said the governor, "the first cross I have seen in this country. Let us adore the Crucified in His image," whereupon they all knelt and said a prayer of gratitude.

After the ceremonies, the governor was asked if he would be godfather to an Indian at Baptism. "Most willingly," he replied. "I am delighted to have the happiness at the beginning of my administration to open the door to a poor soul who wishes to enter Heaven." The governor, accompanied by his officers and the Jesuits, set out for the grimy Indian quarters, where the unsuspecting inhabitants were startled at this invasion of gold and scarlet. The neophyte, who was very sick, answered all the questions satisfactorily. The governor gave him the name of Joseph, and Father Chastellain, entranced at being asked to do so, poured the baptismal water.

The success of that day was heightened when another vessel arrived, bringing two more Jesuits, Father Adam and Brother Cauvet, and forty-three colonists. "It was a beautiful sight," naively remarks the chronicler of the *Relations*, "to see these delicate damosels and the tenderest babes come forth from that prison of wood as day issues from the darkness of night. Notwithstanding all the inconvenience they had to suffer in that floating dwelling, they arrived in as sweet a state of health as if they had been taking a little trip in a carriage."

Charles Garnier was enraptured at these beginnings, and at the near prospect of plunging into the work of the Huron missions. "I am in a Paradise," he wrote to his Carmelite brother, "and in a few days, my happiness will be complete. We are to start for the Huron country." We note also that he thanks Henry for having obtained for him his father's blessing upon his enterprise. Fearful that his father might experience a change of heart with respect to Charles's leaving France for the Huron missions, he had not dared say goodbye to him before setting out for Dieppe and the New World.

On July 1 Garnier and Chastellain departed for Three Rivers. Governor Montmagny escorted them to the shore and ordered three salutes from the cannon as the canoes slipped out into the St. Lawrence.

Father Le Jeune joined them at Three Rivers a week after their arrival there. He had come to arrange with the Huron traders to take the two missionaries to Huronia. While the Jesuits were awaiting the Indians, a squaw with a papoose in her arms appeared at the fort and asked to have the infant baptized, promising to have him reared as a Christian. Garnier administered the sacrament as happily as if the recipient were an Indian chief.

The Hurons touched shore in mid-July and agreed readily to take Garnier and Chastellain with them. To each Indian in the canoes carrying the missionaries a cloak was given, and to each of the two chiefs a blanket, a barrel of peas, and a barrel of bread, together with a supply of prunes. These would have to feed the party for a month, for in their improvidence the Hurons had not cached

away food during their journey. The presents, plus a quantity of tobacco handed them by a missionary whom they met coming down
river, put the Hurons in excellent humor, intensified probably by
the cheerfulness of their Jesuit passengers. In a letter from the
Lake of the Sorcerers, Garnier relates to Le Jeune that the Indians
treated him "like a baby"; they would not let him carry anything
over the portages, not even his own baggage. Only when one of
the Hurons fell sick later on was he permitted to shoulder a burden, but "this was very light," he said. "Indeed, I feel quite depressed because the Lord has not let me bear even a little bit of the
Cross. We reached the Island of the Allumettes on the eve of St.
Ignatius' day; our provisions had given out, and we bought some
corn and reached Lake Nipissing on August 8. There we expect
Father Davost to meet us."

Toward evening of the twelfth, Chastellain's canoe beached below Ihonatiria, and Garnier's one day later. It was the fastest journey yet made by any of the Jesuits, taking three weeks rather than
the usual thirty days. They were greeted warmly by the missionary
veterans. "The joy which is experienced in these reunions," wrote
Le Mercier, "seems to be some image of the happiness of the
blessed upon their arrival in Heaven, it is so full of sweetness. . . .
We gave them a feast; but what a feast! A handful of dried fish and a
little flour. I sent someone out to hunt for a few ears of corn, which
we roasted in the fire. The newcomers said they never had had a
better meal. They declared they felt as if they reached Heaven."

Garnier's cheerful, almost whimsical, state of mind during his
first year of primitive existence in the Huron missions is reflected
in letters to France, which were carefully kept by his brother
Henry, the Carmelite. To his father he wrote, from Ossossané, at a
time in 1637 when he was stricken with the recurrent pestilence
and came close to death:

I am in God's hands, and He takes care of me. Of course, we have persecutions, calumnies, etc., but people of our vocation should never be happy till they hear the Devil crying out against them. As far as I am concerned, there is not a place on earth where I could be more joyous. You ought to know that we have a fortress here that has not its like in France; and our walls are quite different from the Bastille. . . . In fact, our defenses consist only of stakes ten or twelve feet high, and half a foot thick; but we have a tower made of thirty stakes at one corner of this enclosure and on two sides of it. We are going to have two more to protect the two other approaches. Our Hurons fancy that the French forts are built in that fashion. It is only a difference of opinion, and that is one of the reasons I am glad I left France. . . .

You remember how you used to laugh at me because I had no beard. Precisely on that account the savages here think I am a handsome man. You recollect, also, what trouble you had to make me study surgery. Now that is one of my trades here at present, except that it does not go much further than preparing poultices and administering a few harmless drugs. Do not worry about my health. I never felt better in all my life and, indeed, I am convinced that if our friends in France did not develop as much girth as they do, they would be free from many of their ailments. About learning the language, I can assure you that I am making progress, thank God! I jot down every word I hear. I have not the same chance to write as I might have in France, for I am busy from morning till night, instructing, visiting the sick, and receiving the savages in our hut. I am forging ahead, however, but it is hard work to get these poor brutalized people to understand the mysteries of the Faith.

There is no word here of his pestilential sickness, which struck him on September 27. A burning fever sapped his strength, and he fell into a heavy stupor. Without medicines or any physicians, the Jesuits cared for him, then for others of their number who were quickly laid low by the plague, to the limit of their capacities. They prepared a little broth for the sick ones, and tempted their waning appetites with a few raisins and prunes. The aches and fever were aggravated by the noise of the Hurons who thoughtlessly tramped back and forth and around the sickbeds.

When the Indians learned that the Fathers were sick, they flocked boisterously into the cabin, curious to see how the white men would drive out the evil spirits. Some sat cross-legged on the floor all day, watching the faces of the patients; others milled about them, asking for food.

"Please don't shout," said Le Mercier to an Indian near Garnier's bed.

"You have no sense. There is a bird," replied the offended Huron, pointing to a rooster, "that speaks louder than I do, and you say nothing to him."

In spite of the disturbances and the want of medicine, Garnier and the other missionaries recovered, and by mid-October they were nursing the Hurons who now were succumbing.

In the course of these ministrations, Garnier saw in a nearby village his first pagan orgy, which was designed to cure a dying girl. With him was Le Mercier. When they arrived, the squaws began to sing, dance, and perform bodily contortions, while the braves shouted and beat violently on drums of bark. Clouds of suffocating dust rose from the floor, and the heat from the fires grew fiercer. When the chanting and howling had reached a high degree of hysteria, some of the sorcerers took red-hot coals and passed them over the stomach of the patient, who quivered and shook with maniac violence. Then the Indians gorged themselves with food and departed.

The girl lay on her bed limp from exhaustion, and now the missionaries approached her. Le Mercier instructed her briefly in the Christian Faith and proposed Baptism. Thinking at first that Baptism would cure her illness, she was eager to receive it; but when Le Mercier explained its nature more fully, the girl lost interest.

Unwilling to abandon the dying girl, the priests decided to spend the night in the cabin. The patient's fever went higher, and she tossed in delirium. As her relatives looked on suspiciously, the priests took turns praying at her bedside and giving her broth and raisins. In the morning she rallied, her mind cleared, and Le Mercier instructed her further and once more asked if she wanted Baptism. She promptly assented and repeated a few simple prayers, commending her soul to God. Two hours later she died, with the name of Christ on her lips.

This experience convinced Garnier that in spite of the web of superstitions in which the Hurons for centuries had been trapped, tireless work and God's grace could work miracles, as was done in the time of the Apostles. Nothing, he averred, would turn him from this objective. Garnier possessed a full measure of kindness and beguiling charm, and he looked always for the best in others; these qualities gained for him the devotion of the Indians and may even have contributed to his safety and that of his fellow missionaries when the storm of fury broke against them for having presumably, in the minds of the Hurons, brought on the pestilence. Even under these alarming circumstances, even when, at other times, he was confronted with Huron ferocity toward Iroquois captives, Garnier declined to speak harshly of their shortcomings. Thomas J. Campbell remarks of him, "He was a persistent optimist in that, as in everything else, and it may explain how it is that we meet in his life and letters frequent examples of nobility in the savage, which come as a relief in the horrors with which the story of the missions abounds. The Indian was, indeed, very far from being the noble creature such as romance describes him, but he was nevertheless capable of splendid human actions, even before his regeneration by the Faith, but, of course, more than ever when assisted by divine grace."[19]

After two years in Huronia, Charles Garnier had become fluent in the Huron language, and in the summer of 1638 he was assigned to the mission of Ossossané, one of the most populous Huron villages. He had not been there long when a tribe of Indians called the Ouenrohrononnons, of the Neutral family, came to the Hurons for protection. Sick, starving, carrying their meager belongings on their backs, they had traveled one hundred forty miles to Huronia. The Hurons welcomed them and distributed them among the villages. These exiles listened willingly to the gospel, and many embraced Christianity. Garnier's knowledge of medicine proved useful, for numbers of the newly arrived Indians were sick and exhausted, and they were touched by the kindness of the young missionary who brought them back to health.

Garnier, in all his teaching activities, carefully noted the reactions of the Indians to the objects of devotion the missionaries used to assist the catechumens in understanding the Faith. The simple state of the Indian mind is suggested in a letter to his superiors:

> I want a picture of Christ without a beard or with very little, as, for instance, when He was about eighteen years old. On the Cross the figure must be very distinct, and with no one

[19]Thomas J. Campbell, *Pioneer Priests of North America* (New York: The America Press, 1908), Vol. 2, 348.

near Him, so as not to distract attention. Put a crown on the Blessed Virgin, a scepter in her hand, and have our Lord standing on her knee. That quite takes the Indians' fancy. Do not use a halo. They will mistake it for a hat: though rays will answer. In fact, the head must always be uncovered. Send me pictures of the Resurrection, and make the souls of the blessed as happy-looking as possible. Avoid confusion in representing the General Judgment. In the resurrection of the dead, the figures must stand out, and, if possible, let them be illuminated. The faces should not be in profile, but full and with the eyes wide open. The bodies should not be completely draped; at least a part should be bare. There must be no curly hair, and no saint should be bald. Beards also should be debarred, and birds or animals should be kept out of the picture. Our Lord and the Blessed must be very white, and with vivid-colored robes, red, blue, scarlet, but not green or brown. Let the saints coming down from Heaven be as white as snow, with bright garments, and with a happy, smiling countenance, looking affectionately on the spectators and pointing to a motto above: "'The eye hath not seen," etc.

Ready always to see the best in the Indians, Garnier cites a striking instance of brotherly love among the Hurons. A party of Indians from Ossossané were out fishing and were suddenly pounced upon by some roving Iroquois. A young Huron brave fought like a tiger and was careful to protect his little brother, whom the enemy was trying to capture or kill. He managed to keep the boy close to him, and he himself took every blow of the tomahawk or knife. He fell mangled and bleeding over the body of his brother. The enemy, thinking them both dead, withdrew. Garnier found them

huddled together on the river bank, the boy comparatively un-
hurt, but the older one, gasping in death. He knelt beside the
stricken brave, prayed fervently, and saw him regain consciousness.
Garnier instructed him briefly, baptized him, and in a few minutes
the brave expired.

~

In 1639 Charles Garnier was sent to the Petuns, west of
Huronia. From the name of the mission he established, the territory became known as "The Mountains of St. John." The Petuns
have a bewildering variety of names; they are called by at least
twelve in the *Relations*. Once bitter enemies of the Hurons, they
had been driven by the need of safety into an alliance with these
against the common foe, the Iroquois. The Petuns, or Tobacco Indians, traded tobacco, which they grew in abundance, to the Hurons, in exchange for the hatchets and blankets obtained from the
French.

On their first apostolic visit to the Petuns, Garnier and his
companion missionary[20] touched nine villages to each of which
they gave the name of an apostle. They underwent an unceasing
round of hardship, suffering, and great sacrifice. "The mission to
the Petuns," wrote Father Jerome Lalemant to his superior in
France, "was the richest of all, since the crosses and sufferings
there were most abundant."

They set out from Sainte Marie on November 1, stopping off at
Ossossané, where they expected to secure for guide Joseph Chiwatenhwa, a devout Christian Huron. Their hearts sank when
they discovered he was away; from cabin to cabin they went in
search of a guide, and they offered some of their precious supplies

[20]Isaac Jogues.

to anyone who would lead them. None of the braves was willing, however, to undertake the journey in the frightful cold of winter, and the missionaries determined to travel alone.

"With only the good angels for guides," they departed Ossossané. "We reached the principal village, which was called Sts. Peter and Paul, over roads that were altogether too bad for anyone who was not seeking God. Unfortunately, about midway on our journey, we missed a little path which would have led us to some cabins near the main trail, so we had to pass the night in a pine wood. It was a damp place, but we could do no better just then; and with some difficulty we found a few bits of dry wood to make a fire, and some branches to sleep on. There was danger for a time of the snow putting out our fire, but fortunately the storm subsided, and, thanks be to God, we passed the night very comfortably."

The next morning they found the trail again, and they came to a clearing where a few squalid huts were clustered. They hoped to find some food there, but the Indians, themselves impoverished and hungry, were just starting out for the nearest Petun village to replenish their corn supply. The snow covered all the trails now, and the missionaries were glad enough to join these guides providentially supplied them.

Through the deepening snow they trudged, continuing on after dark by the light of its icy glitter, and at eight o'clock they came to a settlement they named St. Thomas. Their only food that day had been a bread crust, and nearly collapsing with hunger, they found a cabin that a brave permitted them to enter. They found an old squaw there who was on the point of death. The Petun language differed only slightly from the Huron, and they were able to give her simple instruction in the Faith and baptize her.

They found that the Petun cabin resembled in all respects the cabins of the Hurons. Five or six fires burned on the earthen floor, and a dozen families huddled among them, sitting, standing, crouching, or lying. Old and young, male and female, children and dogs were mingled.

By the light of the smoky fires, it was an eerie spectacle. Jumping shadows exaggerated the scowling faces and deepened the sidelong glances of suspicion. A senseless and staccato racket smote their ears; frightened children were screaming, and in turn these were clamorously rebuked by the squaws, while the dogs growled and yapped. The missionaries' hosts were by no means cordial, because the Huron accusations against them for bringing on pestilence had re-echoed deep into Petun country, and here the Indians held them to be purveyors of plague and famine.

When the missionaries had quit this settlement and were approaching another village, they could see the squaws gather up their children and hurry off to other places. The braves stood at the cabin doors and scowled at them, threatening the priests if they approached.

One chief was bold enough to invite them. But when he saw them on their knees praying far into the night, he took fright.

"Now I know you are sorcerers," he said. "What do you mean by these postures that we have never seen in this country before?"

No explanation could satisfy him, and he drove them out. Runners preceded them to the next village, warning the inhabitants. Hungry, weary, the wayfarers could get no food, and until nightfall they had nothing to eat. They fell in with a band of refugee Neutrals, and these allowed them to baptize "a little monster" of a baby. "The poor little misshapen thing," they wrote, "became an angel."

They came to a village and found shelter in a cabin where a feast to a demon was taking place. For hours the Indians practiced incantations and nonsensical dances and threw gobs of tobacco into the fire. They were attempting to cure a sick person who had not fulfilled the injunctions of a dream.

That shelter was temporary, too, and the next morning the missionaries again set forth on their weary tramp. Hostility increased as they wandered from village to village. If they were taken into a wigwam, at midnight sullen mobs would gather outside and order the Blackrobes out. In one instance, a savage jumped up from his sleep and drove them forth into the dark. Through snow, rain, ice, and cold they would slog on to another village, and there an angry brave would lift his tomahawk, promising to brain them if they tried to enter.

One of the Fathers — we do not know which — fell sick; while he was convalescing, both were driven out of the sheltering wigwam at three o'clock in the morning. They had a handful of bread with them, and "such bread," remarks Le Mercier, "you would not give to a dog in France."

In the face of these relentless setbacks, here and there the priests were able to accomplish some spiritual good among the stray Indians they encountered, and this, in their estimation, was an adequate reward.

Meanwhile, back in Ossossané, rumors reached the Christian Huron Joseph Chiwatenhwa that the missionaries were undergoing serious difficulties with the Petuns. Joseph, a member of one of the leading families, was a man whose personal attributes placed him high among the Hurons. He had taken long and detailed instructions from the Jesuits, and at about the age of thirty-five he was baptized, on August 15, 1638. His gifts of mind and character were so marked that the missionaries considered him comparable to the more talented men to be found in France. He grasped thoroughly the teachings of the Fathers, and his acute memory permitted him never to forget a word he had learned from them. He married young, remained faithful to his wife, and chose to refrain from gambling, drinking, and even smoking. He attached high importance to personal discipline. Joseph mastered reading and writing, and he persuaded all of his family to accept the Faith. He enjoyed a strategic situation in combating the ungrounded beliefs and deplorable morality of the Indians, and his unique example operated more powerfully than even his reasoned and passionate arguments in spreading the Faith through the wigwams.

When Joseph heard that things were going badly with the Petun missionaries, he promptly declared, "I will go there." His wife entreated him to stay home, fearing he would never return. He reassured her and set forth into a raging snowstorm. The trees were cracking and splitting, the sharp wind was blowing the snow into mountainous drifts, but no conditions of weather could corrode his iron determination to reach the missionaries. He found them, and he tried to find shelter for the Blackrobes among relatives of his. These, too, had been inflamed against the travelers; reproaching Joseph for accompanying the sorcerers, they closed their doors to all three. Joseph did find quarters for the night, but a young brave of the village declared he was going to kill the Blackrobes and set out with his tomahawk to do so. Fortunately the missionaries had changed sleeping quarters, and while the excited Petun was hunting about for them, Joseph intercepted and disarmed him.

The following day the little party headed for the large settlement of Sts. Peter and Paul, which they had earlier visited. Here they were rebuffed again, and angry squaws screamed out, "Where are the braves who said they would kill these men if they returned?" Admitted for the night to one cabin, they were driven out into the blackness and later were pursued by a band of Petuns with tomahawks. These Indians missed the trail, and the next day the village chief caught up with the missionaries and expressed regret for what had happened.

Indignantly, Joseph replied, "It is not these Blackrobes who are disturbing the country; it is you, who will not listen to the important things they have to tell you. You laugh at me and call me 'The Believer.' That is my greatest glory. You know me, and you know my people. I am proud to follow the teachings of these great men. Our ancestors were excusable, for they never heard what you have heard, but you will be punished a thousand times worse than they if you persist in the degradation from which the missionaries wish to raise you."

The old Petun chief heard him out in chastened silence and grunted, "True," then adroitly changed the subject.

Throughout that long and terrible winter, Garnier and his companion had labored with patience and determination among the Petuns. They had endured every hardship without complaining. Yet, although they had braved their way into some three hundred reluctant cabins, they had not won a single convert in good health. They had accomplished this much, however: they had baptized a substantial number of sick and dying Indians, and they had provided the surly Petuns with an example of unconquerable fortitude. They had done all that human courage and sacrifice could do; the rest was in the hands of God. With cheerful confidence they left the issue in His hands and trudged back, haggard and exhausted, to Ossossané. Of them, Parkman observes, "Nowhere is the power of courage, faith, and an unflinching purpose more strikingly displayed than in the record of these missions."

A few months after Garnier returned to Ossossané, Joseph Chiwatenhwa was commissioned to carry a letter to the Jesuits at Quebec. On the evening of August 2, 1640, he had gone into the woods to cut saplings for the boat that was to take him there.

Three of his little nieces had followed him, but at the edge of the woods he stopped them.

"There are too many dangers lurking in the woods," he said. "Kneel and say a few prayers, and then go home."

They carried out his bidding, and he entered the forest. Two Iroquois crept up stealthily behind him. One of them plunged a javelin into his body while the other struck him in the head with a tomahawk and tore off his scalp.

There was great sorrow in Ossossané, especially, among the missionaries, for they had lost a valiant Christian warrior and a fellow missionary whose holiness of life and deep, living faith were unparalleled among the Indians of Huronia.

That fall, Charles Garnier, accompanied by Father Pierre Pijart, ventured forth in another effort to evangelize the intractable Petuns. In accordance with the suggestion of their superior, Jerome Lalemant, when they arrived in the Petun country, they asked for a general meeting of the chiefs; they wished to explain the purpose of their mission and to dissipate the charges that were mainly responsible for their previous difficulties. After considerable delay and prevarication, the chiefs arranged a council. Garnier was spokesman for the missionary cause, and he explained graphically and beguilingly that he and his companion had come to teach them the truth concerning Him-who-made-all and to show them the way to eternal life.

But the Hurons again had gotten in their work. Fearful that the Petuns might encroach upon their trade with the French if the Petuns became friendly with the Blackrobes, they had spread further calumnies, charging the missionaries with being sorcerers determined to annihilate the Indians with the pestilence, and urging that they not be received in the villages. The campaign bore fruit. The chiefs refused the presents the Blackrobes had brought for them, and they expressed clear hostility to the mission. Some clamored for the scalps of the intruders, but others were content to make no objection to sheltering them in their villages.

Undaunted by the general antagonism toward them, Garnier and Pijart determined to take their chances, and they started off on their rounds. During that winter, their experiences were comparable to those of the winter before, but they did fare somewhat better in certain places. One village, whose chief had warned the missionaries that to visit there would mean death, welcomed them with genuine enthusiasm.

On their travels, one adventure occurred that was to mystify them to the end of their numbered days. They were emerging from a forest waist-deep in snow, packs on their backs, when without warning they felt heavy hands on their shoulders and heard a wild scream: "You are dead!" They were flung onto their backs and expected the tomahawk at any moment. Nothing happened. They struggled to their feet and were amazed to see a number of Indians, stark naked, scampering off in all directions.

Later on they narrated the incident at Sainte Marie, and it was suggested they had accidentally stumbled upon some forest incantation ceremony and probably had surprised the Indians as much as they were surprised themselves. The missionaries could not refrain from cogitating upon what demon was so trying a taskmaster as to demand such scant covering for his devotees in the dead of winter.

Garnier, always alert to the virtues of others, related how, when a band of Petuns were trudging through the deep snow that covered a frozen lake in the bitter cold, a girl in the party showed clear signs of collapsing. Instantly her brother stripped the furs from his own shoulders and wrapped them about her. Then, to overcome her numbness, he forced her to run. She reached her destination, but he fell dead in the snow, frozen to death. Garnier relates several instances of like devotion among the Indians, and these stories provide relief from the recurrent horrors of that country.

The *Relations* do not enable us to follow Garnier year by year after this second expedition to the Petuns. We know this, that he labored among the various Huron missions and everywhere won over the Indians by precept and example, and the other missionaries by good humor and unflagging dedication to his work. To his confreres, Thomas J. Campbell remarks, "He was an angel, forever walking in the presence of God." We learn, from the *Relations* that Garnier could step into the midst of a savage brawl among the Indians and quickly restore peace and order, so commanding was his quiet authority. He could take hold of a raving maniac, even, and bring him to his senses.

Of the letters that Charles Garnier wrote to his father and two of his brothers, mostly from the Huron missions, twenty-four have been preserved. They breathe a spirit of unwavering piety and of selfless conformity to God's will. His love for his family and solicitude for their well-being are present always. To his brother Joseph, at this period still the wayward member of the family, he writes from Ossossané, "Just today I said Mass for you, and as always it was with a great love for you. If I could give my life blood to help you, I would do so. If I were called upon to leave this mission, which I consider an earthly paradise, and if God's will and my superiors should wish it, I would gladly return to you in France if my return could be of any help. God knows how much I wish to help you. I have offered to Him the sacrifice of my life for your conversion. I have consecrated my whole being to Him, to do as He wills with me, so that He may win you back."

Later, writing from the Island of St. Joseph to both brothers, Henry the Carmelite and Joseph-turned-Capuchin, at a time when his own martyrdom was not far off, he says, "This little letter is to encourage all three of us to increase our love for our divine Master, because I cannot help but think that one of us is very near the end of his career. Let us, therefore, redouble our fervor, let us hasten our steps, let us make a new pact that whichever one of us three our Lord calls first will be an advocate for the two left behind, to obtain for them a deep love of our Lord, a closer union with Him, and final perseverance. I, then, first make this pact and pray our Lord with all my heart to take possession of our three hearts and make them one with His own, now and for all eternity."

Father Francis Bressani relates that Garnier thought nothing of walking thirty or forty miles on the hottest summer day to baptize some dying Indian, when the woods were infested with Iroquois. On such errands he would sometimes pass the night alone in the forest in the dead of winter, reclining on pine branches. The *Relations* depict him carrying sick people on his back — and he was not the strongest of men — for distances of up to six miles to gain the opportunity of baptizing them. Far from dreading an encounter with the Iroquois, "he often told us," says Father Ragueneau, "that he would be quite content to fall into the hands of the Iroquois and remain their prisoner if, while they were torturing him, he at least had a chance of instructing them as long as his torments lasted. If they allowed him to live, it would afford him a golden opportunity to work for their conversion, which was now impossible, since the gateway to their country was closed as long as they were our enemies."

In the winter of 1647, Garnier and Father Leonard Garreau went back to the petuns, and they founded two missions there, near the Huron border, in the villages of Ekarreniondi and Etarita, which they named respectively St. Matthias and St. John. They built a chapel in each village, and they found the natives more responsive than ever they had been on Garnier's two expeditions earlier. The priests won to Baptism one hundred eighty-four Petuns.

Meanwhile the depredations of the Iroquois were becoming more frequent and disastrous. In July 1648, they wiped out the village of Teanaustayé,[21] and in November 1649, some Hurons, returning to their own country from the Petuns, reported the alarming news that the Iroquois were on the warpath against those people and were boasting that soon they would burn their villages to the ground.

At this time there were four priests among the Petuns: Fathers Grelon and Garreau were some twelve miles from the Huron border, in the hills of the Petuns; and in the frontier village of Etarita was Charles Garnier, who had been joined by the young Jesuit missionary Noël Chabanel.

[21] See chapter 10.

~

Chapter 12

Noël Chabanel was the youngest and the last of the eight Jesuit martyrs of North America to die. For him, the sojourn among the Indians was a singularly difficult odyssey of the flesh and of the spirit. As St. Joseph is mentioned rarely in the Gospels but stands in the background always, so Chabanel is little mentioned in the *Relations*; his conquests, heroic in quality, were achieved over himself even more prominently than over the paganism in whose toils he labored, and his final victory burns with a special luster.

He was born February 2, 1613, near Mende, Toulouse, in the south of France, a short time after the Huguenots had devastated that region. Entering the Society of Jesus in 1630 at the age of seventeen, he followed the usual courses of philosophy and theology, and he taught these subjects for five years. In 1643 he set sail for New France, having been attracted strongly to the Canadian missions. He had proved himself to be a scholar of superior attainment; he had taught French literature at Rhodez and Toulouse and shown a marked turn for poetry. If he had remained in France, it seems probable he would have distinguished himself as an orator and man of letters.

With him on the vessel were two other Jesuits, the venerable Father Claude Quentin and the young Father Leonard Garreau. They were three months on the water, and it was with unspeakable relief that they put in at the harbor of Quebec on August 15.

The St. Lawrence River was swarming with Iroquois that summer, and it was impossible to make the journey to Huronia until the following year, and even when that time came, the project was risky. The governor made up his mind to force a passage, and he assigned twenty-two soldiers to accompany Chabanel, two other Jesuits, and the party of about sixty Hurons. It is related that the wilder lads among the soldiery, who had at first looked upon the trip as a lark, were distinctly sobered by the rigors of the journey.

They arrived at Sainte Marie on September 7, 1644. Here Noël Chabanel applied himself energetically to the study of Huron. His intelligence was keen, his memory excellent, but he made little headway with this barbarous language, which differed so radically from his beloved, highly developed mother tongue. The sounds and structure were a torment to him, and his failure, at first a worry, grew into a galling of the mind and a wracking of the nerves. To add poignancy to his frustration, his sensitive nature revolted against the grossness and filth of the Hurons, and there developed in his heart a loathing for them. A short stay in one of their cabins would befoul him with dirt and excrement, nauseate him with its putrid stench, and deafen him with the pandemonium of children, squaws, and dogs. The sight of their food, scarcely less than its taste, repelled him, and only with revulsion could he swallow it. His whole nature recoiled from the indelicate rawness of this existence.

These things were bad enough; what alarmed him, however, was that the heroic sentiments that formerly had animated him seemed to be vanishing under the dull blows of this savage life. He did not now yearn for martyrdom as his fellow missionaries did; rather, he experienced a growing dread of being tortured and burned alive. It is not difficult to sympathize with him in this matter.

The *Relations* say that "he could not adjust himself to the customs of the country, nor to the life of the missions, which was so radically opposed to his natural inclinations and was for him all suffering without any consoling feature. He had always to lie on bare ground, to live from morning to night in a little hell of smoke and in places that were often filled with snow in the morning [the snow came into the Indian cabins from every side], to live in dwellings filled with vermin, where each sense had its own particular torture day and night. He never had pure water with which to quench his thirst, while the best food he had to eat was generally a paste made of Indian corn ground and boiled in water. He had to work incessantly, ever underfed and without a single moment when he could retire to some place that was not entirely public. He had no bedroom of his own, no office, no study, no light other than that of a smoky fire, surrounded by ten to fifteen people, crowded around by children of all ages, screaming, crying, and quarreling. He had to dwell in a congested room where people washed and cooked, ate, worked, and attended to everything else that is done in a household."

Chabanel sank into a deep depression of spirits. In France he could have accomplished much for the honor of God and the salvation of souls, but life in this fabulous wilderness was all mortification, frustration, loathing, and mental torment. Even after he had wrestled with the language for four years, he could speak it only wretchedly. His embarrassment became all the while more chafing, and he was sometimes moved to throw in the sponge. "Return to France," whispered the tempter. "You have been under a delusion. You have no vocation for this work. Your superiors have made a frightful mistake. You belong in the colleges of France, where your literary talents will bring a rich harvest and win you the recognition every scholar welcomes as a spur to still greater achievement." Whispered in his ear day after day and month after month was the refrain, and it finally became so powerful and so clamorous that it taxed all his strength to resist it.

Father Paul Ragueneau, Superior of Sainte Marie, perceived the struggle Chabanel was undergoing within him. He alludes to the physical conditions that were breeding the young Jesuit's aversion, then turns the light into the soul of Chabanel: "When, in addition, God withdraws His visible graces and remains hidden, although a person sighs for Him alone, and when He leaves the soul a prey to sadness, disgust, and natural aversions — these are the trials which are greater than ordinary virtue can bear. The love of God has to be strong in the heart not to be snuffed out under such circumstances. Add to this the danger, present at every moment of the day, of being attacked by a savage enemy armed with fire and flames and unheard-of torments, who would more often force you to suffer a thousand deaths before you met death itself. One certainly had to have the strength of the sons of God not to lose courage in the midst of such desolation."

To return to France, to devote his life to civilized people in an environment of culture, was what Chabanel's nature passionately craved with growing insistence. At last, faced with a crisis so fundamental, he firmly and irrevocably made his choice. He would stay at his post of duty, even though it surely meant a new crucifixion each day. He would stay on at his work: He could say Mass; he could baptize; he could speak to the savages, although haltingly, of the truths of religion; he could teach them by an example of interior fortitude that certainly they could sense. The boulders of suffering that stood out before him he would transform into stepping stones to a life of close union with God and of acquiescence in His will. He would do all he could, and God would take care of the rest.

Father Ragueneau penetratingly tells how the temptation of Noël Chabanel was overcome: "It was in this complete gloom that God wished to try the fidelity of this good Father for five or six years. Nevertheless, the Devil never made any headway in his numerous attacks, although every day he tried to show the Father that by returning to France he would find the joy, rest, and consolation which had always been his in the past. He suggested that Father Chabanel would find plenty of work in France more suited to his talents, and that any number of holy people there practiced the virtues of charity and zeal for souls to a high degree and spent their entire lives working for the salvation of their neighbor. Yet, he never wished to come down from the cross upon which God had placed him, nor did he ever ask for an easy way out. On the contrary, in order to bind himself more irrevocably to his cross, he obligated himself by vow to remain on it for life and to die there."

With this vow Chabanel put beyond himself all further thought of abandoning his missionary purpose:

My Lord, Jesus Christ, who by the admirable dispositions of Divine Providence hast willed that I should be a helper of the holy apostles of this Huron vineyard, entirely unworthy though I be, drawn by the desire to cooperate with the designs which the Holy Ghost has upon me for the conversion of the savage Hurons to the Faith; I, Noël Chabanel, in the presence of the Blessed Sacrament of Thy Sacred Body and Most Precious Blood, which is the Testament of God with man; I vow perpetual stability in this Huron Mission; it being understood that all this is subject to the dictates of the Superiors of the Society of Jesus, who may dispose of me as they wish. I pray, then, O Lord, that Thou wilt deign to accept me as a permanent servant in this mission and that Thou wilt render me worthy of so sublime a ministry. Amen. The twentieth day of June 1647.

It was the feast of Corpus Christi. Chabanel's natural revulsion toward the Indian village life was not to leave him, but before his irrevocable ultimatum, and with God's grace, he beat back every temptation and gained the perseverance for which he ardently prayed.

That the *Relations* report little of Noël Chabanel's ministry to the Indians, of the places to which he ventured, and of the episodes that attended his career, we need not greatly regret; for his peculiar interest to us resides in the magnificent drama that developed within his own soul, and of this we have ample information. We know that he traveled among the Huron missions generally[22] and that Father Ragueneau's assignments for the winter of 1647 list him with Sainte Marie. He also worked among the roving Algonquins. He reveals one interesting assignment in a letter to his Jesuit brother, Pierre Chabanel, in France, and humor is not absent from his thoughts:

Your Reverence missed, by a very narrow margin, having a brother a martyr. But, alas, before God one must have virtue of a different kind to mine before meriting the honor of martyrdom. Father Gabriel Lalemant,[23] one of the three whom our *Relations* say have suffered for Christ, had replaced me

[22]With Jean de Brébeuf.
[23]See chapter 9.

at the village of St. Louis just a month before his death, while I, being stronger, was sent to a more distant and more difficult mission, but one not so fertile in palms and crowns as the one for which my laxity rendered me unworthy before God. My turn will come when it pleases the Divine Bounty, provided that I, for my part, try to live a "bloodless" martyr in the shadow of martyrdom. The ravages of the Iroquois upon this country will probably sometime do the rest for me, through the merits of so many saints, among whom I have the consolation of living peacefully in the midst of so much confusion and continual danger to one's life.

The *Relations* make it unnecessary for me to add anything to what I have said. Besides, I have only enough of paper and time to beg Your Reverence and all the Fathers of your Province to remember me at the altar, as a victim probably destined for the fires of the Iroquois, "that through the intercession of the saints I may merit such a great victory in so great a struggle."

And now, in the fall of 1649, he was sent to the frontier village of Etarita to assist Father Charles Garnier in evangelizing the Petuns. When he was preparing to leave, he remarked to Father Chastellain, who was his spiritual director, "This time I hope to give myself to God once and for all, and to belong entirely to Him." Chastellain, meeting one of the Fathers a little later, observed, "I have just been deeply moved. That good Father spoke to me with the look and voice of a victim offering up his sacrifice. I do not know what God has in store for him, but I can see that He wants him to be a great saint."

Chabanel himself unburdened his thoughts to a friend: "I do not know what is happening to me, nor how God wishes to use me, but I feel entirely changed on one point. I am naturally very apprehensive, yet, now that I am going into greater danger than ever before and feel that death is not far off, I am not in the least afraid. This frame of mind does not come from myself."

Conditions at Etarita were considerably worse than any that Chabanel had so far experienced. Although the persevering Garnier had won over a generous number of Petuns to Christianity, hostility was not absent among many of the Indians of that region, and their squalor was shocking to Chabanel's sensibilities; nevertheless he braved them courageously. But these circumstances dwindled in importance in the face of the widening danger from the Iroquois, now bent on crushing the Petuns.

This danger was great enough to prompt Father Ragueneau to direct that three of the four missionaries with the Petuns should return to Sainte Marie, which had been transferred to the large Island of St. Joseph, near Sault Sainte Marie, upon which converged the lakes of Superior, Michigan, and Huron. It was November 1649 when Ragueneau learned of the growing Iroquois depredations.

Chabanel and Garnier had been together not many weeks, although in those weeks were concentrated almost stupefying hardships and perils, and their food had largely consisted of roots and acorns. The veteran Garnier in particular was weary. His accomplishments among the Petuns had been considerable, and now he was held in high respect by most of these people. Since summer of that year, his flock had been swollen by Hurons who had fled the slaughter at Ossossané, and Garnier was wearing himself out in ministering to the increased numbers. After spending an entire day in traveling from cabin to cabin, tending the sick and instructing catechumens, he would think nothing of rising in the dead of night to travel ten or twenty miles to the bedside of a dying Indian, baptizing him or giving the last sacraments.

Even with Chabanel beside him in the mission at Etarita, the work was unceasing, and it was with no light heart that, in pursuance of Father Ragueneau's order, he executed the difficult task of directing Noël to return to Sainte Marie. His own mood at this time is expressed in a letter to Ragueneau dated December 4: "I have no fears about my health. What I should fear more would be that of deserting my flock in their misery of hunger and amidst the terrors of war, since they have need of me more than ever. I would fail to use the opportunity which God gives me of losing myself for Him, and so render myself unworthy of His favors. . . . At all times I am ready to leave everything and die in the spirit of obedience."

On Sunday, December 5, Noël Chabanel celebrated Mass and said farewell to Garnier. "I am going," he said, "to where obedience calls me, but whether I stay there or receive permission from my superior to return to the mission where I belong, I must serve God faithfully until death." The chronicler of the *Relations* comments, "But God willed that, as they had lived and labored together in the same mission, they should not be separated in death." Chabanel departed in the company of a small group of Christian Hurons who thought it wiser to escape to other parts than to wait for the impending Iroquois attack on Etarita.

A formidable band of Petun warriors set forth from Etarita, intending to take by surprise the three hundred Iroquois reported marching toward the village. But the Iroquois circled wide and, slipping quietly through the forest, escaped the Petun searching party. When they reached the vicinity of Etarita, they captured a Petun brave and his squaw and learned from the frightened couple that the village had comparatively few defenders.

On Tuesday, December 7, 1649, at three o'clock in the afternoon, Charles Garnier was making his usual rounds in the village when suddenly the shout was heard: "The Iroquois! The Iroquois!"

The invaders, with terrifying war cries, streamed through the gates and slashed down men, women, and children. The few Petun braves still in the village made a show of resistance but were quickly overwhelmed by the furious Iroquois onslaught.

To the Christians who ran to him, Father Garnier called out, "My brothers, we are dead men! Pray to God, and take flight! Escape any way you can! Go quickly! Keep your faith as long as you live! May death find you thinking of God!" Then he pronounced general absolution over them.

To Garnier the Petuns shouted, "Save yourself! Escape with us!" There still was time, but it was not for him to abandon his people, and he waved them on. He hurried into several of the cabins which already were aflame and ministered to the terrified occupants. The Iroquois, swinging their tomahawks and howling like fiends, closed in upon him. A bullet penetrated his breast and another ripped open his stomach. He fell, writhing in agony, and the enemy pounced on him, tore his cassock from his body, and left him naked and bleeding.

He came back to consciousness a little later, and he saw a Petun brave squirming in pain a short distance away. Struggling to help this man, perhaps to baptize him with melted snow, he crawled a few feet and fell. Blood was issuing from his wounds, and his strength was failing rapidly. Death was ready to close in, but Garnier's passionate concern for souls, which had filled his waking hours, still throbbed, driving him on, and it was stronger than death. He raised himself to his knees and crawled a few paces on hands and knees toward the dying Petun. At that moment, according to the testimony of a squaw who had concealed herself nearby, an Iroquois swooped down upon him, scalped him, and plunged his tomahawk through each temple and buried it deep in the brain. The hand that was stretched out to aid an unknown

Petun Indian fell limp. It was his last act, and it was the perfect symbol of his whole apostolate.

The Iroquois hurried their work of destruction, fearful that the absent warriors might return in time to take revenge. They scattered firebrands right and left, and into the flaming cabins they threw little children snatched from their mothers' arms. Soon Etarita was a smoldering ruin.

The Iroquois left the ashes of the village, heading toward Huronia, where already they had advanced far in extirpating the population. They herded along with them all captives able to walk, butchering those who lagged. One Christian mother was killed because she wept for her massacred child.

Twelve miles away, in the Petun village of St. Matthias, the inhabitants read the tragic story in the smoke that towered from the burning cabins. It was a night of anguish and suspense for St. Matthias, where Fathers Garreau and Grelon were. In the morning, scouts brought word that the enemy had left, and the two priests hurried to the scene. The ghastly spectacle filled them with horror. Mangled corpses littered the bloodstained snow; bodies charred beyond recognition lay among the remains of the cabins. In a few bodies a spark of life still lingered. In the center of the village they saw a naked corpse, splashed with blood and blackened by the ashes and mud in which it lay. They passed on, but the keen eyes of the Indians recognized it, and the priests were called back.

It was indeed the body of Charles Garnier. They washed it in the snow and removed their own garments to cover it. They dug a shallow grave where his chapel had stood, and with grief-laden hearts they recited the funeral prayers and lowered the body to its earthly resting place. "The poverty of the burial was great," wrote Father Ragueneau, "but the sacredness was no less marked." Later on, when the Iroquois were no longer close by, they would rescue his bones.

Two days afterward the Petun war party returned home. When they saw the grim evidence of the tragedy, they sat down among their dead. They stared at the ground in silence, without even a moan, grieving for their wives and children. Half a day they sat, in soundless lamentation.

Noël Chabanel and his Huron companions reached St. Matthias on the same day they had left Etarita, December 5. He spent two nights with Garreau and Grelon, leaving on the morning of the seventh for the Island of St. Joseph. This was some hours before the Iroquois attack on Etarita, which occurred in the afternoon. Seven or eight Hurons accompanied him. Darkness overtook them after they had traveled eighteen miles over difficult trails, and they lay down to rest in a dense woodland at a place where the Nottawasaga makes a great bend before it empties into the bay of that name.

The Hurons quickly fell asleep, but Father Chabanel remained awake and prayed. Toward midnight he heard a confused mur-mur in the distance; then more clearly came the war songs of the victorious Iroquois and the cries of their captives as the procession approached. Chabanel awakened the Hurons, who took flight, circling the enemy and heading back toward St. Matthias.

Chabanel, worn out from fatigue and hunger, followed along for a little while and then, realizing he could no longer keep up, fell on his knees and said to them, "It matters not if I die. Life is but a slight thing after all, and the Iroquois cannot rob me of Par-adise." They left him there and continued on to St. Matthias, where they reported what had taken place.

It appears that when day broke, Chabanel had given up all thought of returning to St. Matthias, and he resumed his journey to the Island of St. Joseph. He reached a river, but it was too deep to ford. An Indian found him bareheaded there and, as he reported later, took him across in his canoe. According to the *Relations*, the Indian declared that "in order to escape more rapidly, the Father had thrown away his coat and the sack which contained his notes and a blanket that served our missionaries as overcoat and mantle, mattress and coverlet, bed and all other furniture, even as a dwelling when they are in the country without any shelter."

Noël Chabanel never reached the Island of St. Joseph. For some time the exact nature of his fate remained obscure. But the Fathers came to suspect strongly that the Huron who took him across the river had robbed and killed him. "This man," reports Father Ragueneau, referring to the Huron, "had been a Christian and since had become an apostate and was quite capable of clubbing the Father and throwing his body into the river in order to rob him of his possessions. If we had wanted to follow up the affair, I believe we could have found convincing evidence against this murderer, but, in this time of public calamity, we thought it better to stifle our suspicions and close our eyes to something we did not want to see. Our only concern is in the service of God."

Two years later the suspicions of the missionaries were to be confirmed. In a note to the *Relation* of 1652, Ragueneau states, "A trustworthy Christian told us that he had heard the man, from his own lips, boasting that he was the murderer, and that he had rid the world of the carrion Frenchman, that he had brained him at his own feet and had thrown the body into the river." This Huron apostate, Louis Honareenhax, acknowledged he had done so through hatred of the Faith. He had renounced Christianity because misfortunes befell him; he bitterly hated the missionaries and had publicly announced his intention to kill one of them.

Noël Chabanel's death in the gloom of the forest, where he was alone with his killer, recalls the strange presentiment which he had expressed in a letter to his brother: "Perhaps I shall be a martyr in the darkness and undergo a bloodless martyrdom."

Compared with the physical tortures that accompanied the death of Brébeuf or of Gabriel Lalemant, Chabanel's were trifling. But in the lasting inner turmoil of his years in the mission country, in the loathing and the revulsion of spirit, in the mental torment of life with the Indians, Chabanel underwent a martyrdom more protracted and more excruciating than did all the others. Every day was an agony for his sensibilities; his first years in New France were a train of unrelenting temptations to give up his struggle, but his dogged determination overrode every inclination to veer away from the straight road to martyrdom. Noël Chabanel's body was never recovered, but his memory lives on as the last of the eight who gave their lives in the missions of the New World.

The companion of Chabanel's last few weeks, Charles Garnier, the indomitable veteran of the Huron and Petun missions, died on December 7, 1649, the day before his younger confrere. The news did not reach Father Ragueneau at Sainte Marie until the twelfth, when it was brought to him by the Hurons who had set out with Chabanel. The shock to Ragueneau was mollified by the thought that Garnier was surely in Heaven. He wrote a report to the Jesuit provincial in France, saying:

> I had known him for over twelve years. . . . I can truthfully say that in all that time I do not think he was ever a single hour, except when asleep, without an ardent desire of advancing more and more in the way of God and of seeing his neighbor advance along the same path. . . . God was

everything to him and, without God, everything was as nothing. . . . His virtues were heroic, and he was not lacking in a single one that goes to make up a great saint. His obedience was very solid, and he was ready to do anything or remain idle if the superiors wished it so. . . . He mortified himself night and day, always sleeping on a hard bed and carrying on his body some part of the cross, which he cherished in life and upon which he hoped to meet his death. Each time he came back from his mission, he made sure to sharpen anew the iron points of the belt which he wore next to his skin. More than that, he often used an iron discipline, also studded with sharp points. His food was the food of the Indians, that is, less than any miserable beggar in France would expect to have. During this last winter's famine, acorns and bitter roots were his delicacies. . . .

Those in greatest need were the object of his tenderest solicitude. No matter how disgusting a person's manners were, nor how mean and impudent his actions, he loved all with the love of a mother and never neglected any corporal work of mercy that would help for the salvation of souls. He would dress ulcers that were so poisoned and infectious that the Indians, even the nearest relatives of the patient, could not force themselves to dress them. Alone he would undertake the task of swabbing away the pus and dressing the wound every day for two or three months, exercising the greatest care and tenderness, although often he knew well that the wounds were incurable. "But," he would say, "the more fatal the wounds, the more I am inclined to nurse them in order to bring these poor people to the gates of Heaven and to prevent them from falling into sin at the most dangerous time of their lives."

From early childhood, Charles Garnier had a special devotion to the Blessed Virgin, whom he called his mother. "It is she," he once said, "who carried me in her arms through my youth and placed me in the Society of her Son." He had taken a vow to uphold until his death the belief in her Immaculate Conception, not at that time declared formally a dogma of the Catholic Church. It was on the vigil of this feast that he died, at the age of forty-four.

Book Six

The Curtain Falls

~

Chapter 13

The story of the Jesuit martyrs of North America is so closely inter-twined with the Hurons, upon whom they concentrated their greatest efforts, that it scarcely seems complete without an account of the fate that befell that once mighty nation. The one is insepara-ble from the other.

The Huron population was dwindling at an alarming rate. The bullets and tomahawks of the Iroquois had killed hundreds, but famine, influenza, and smallpox had killed thousands. Champlain, in 1615, and the Récollets and Brébeuf, in 1626, had estimated the Huron population at thirty thousand. Brébeuf confirmed this estimate as late as 1636. But a survey that he and the other mis-sionaries conducted in the summer of 1640 revealed seven hun-dred longhouses and two thousand fires and placed the total population at twelve thousand. This decline, if continued, indi-cated extermination in a very few years.

Within a few weeks of Brébeuf's death in March 1649, fifteen Huron villages were abandoned. St. Louis and St. Ignace were re-duced to ashes, and the great settlement at Ossossané was deserted. In panic and consternation, the Bear tribe fled to the land of the

Petuns. Hundreds from the other tribes that made up the Huron confederacy sought refuge among the Neutrals, to the south, and still others journeyed to the western nation of the Eries, but both throngs of refugees shared the disasters that overcame those two tribes. Hundreds of families found temporary haven in the nearby islands, and even greater numbers fled to the Algonquins; other Hurons reached the Andastes. The inhabitants of two villages, St. Michel and St. Jean Baptiste, had recourse to a desperate although not unique expedient: they petitioned the Senecas, a constituent nation of the Iroquois confederacy, for refuge, and in return they promised to forsake their own nationality and become Senecas. Their proposal was accepted, and along with Hurons from a few other localities, they migrated in a body to the Seneca country. They were not distributed among various settlements, but were permitted to form their own village, where they were soon joined by some prisoners of the Neutral nation.

While the refugees identified themselves with the Iroquois and followed their lead in virtually all matters, they held fast to their faith; eighteen years later, a Jesuit missionary was astonished to find them steadfast in their Christian beliefs and practices.

And in such a manner were the remnants of a race, whose forward strides in agriculture seemed to stamp them for dominance among all Indians, scattered among alien tribes. Their villages were silent, their cabins in ruin, their homeland deserted, save for the hundreds who camped about Sainte Marie.

Scarcely less desolate than the Hurons were Father Paul Ragueneau and his fellow missionaries. Huronia depopulated, they must follow as they could their dispersed flocks. This necessitated a most painful decision: they must abandon and destroy Fort Sainte Marie, the center of their entire missionary enterprise and the place which had become endeared to them by years of association.

A new center would have to be founded, and they determined upon the island of Ekaentoton, named by them Sainte Marie, one hundred eighty miles to the north, and beyond reach of the Iroquois. It was a gateway to Lake Superior and the nations of the west, and it offered easy passage to the route to Quebec. Furthermore, a considerable number of Hurons were already building a village there. But at this time, twelve Huron elders called upon the Jesuits at the Sainte Marie mission and announced that the Huron people were once more becoming a united nation and had made up their minds to erect a great and impregnable village on the island of Ahoendoe, called by the missionaries the Island of St. Joseph, which was not far from Ekaentoton. The elders begged the missionaries not to desert them in their need, but to unite with them at St. Joseph and save their nation.

"We could not doubt," reported Ragueneau, "that God had chosen to speak to us by their lips. Although at their coming we had decided upon another plan, we all found ourselves changed before their departure. By unanimous consent we agreed that it was necessary to follow God in the direction whither He chose to call us — for the remaining future — whatever peril there might be in it for us, in whatever depth of darkness we might continue." On the Island of St. Joseph, separated by only a channel from the Huron country, they would build a new Sainte Marie.

Since the Iroquois might swoop down upon them at any moment, they wasted no time and soon were feverishly at work. Carpenters built a barge twenty feet long and a raft about forty-five feet long. Bundling their clothes, packaging their provisions, and wrapping up their sacred vessels, they carried down to barge and raft all they could safely assemble upon them and destroyed the rest. At five o'clock on Monday morning, June 14, apprised by scouts that there were no Iroquois lurking in the woods, Father

Ragueneau uttered probably the most difficult order of his life: "Put the torch to Sainte Marie."

They pushed out into the bay and looked with unashamed tears at the clouds of smoke and the tongues of flame that leapt into the sky. Their beloved Sainte Marie — chapel, community residence, longhouses, barns, sheds, palisades — a bastion of the Faith in the American wilderness, would soon be ashes. "We have left our dwelling place," Ragueneau wrote, "rather I might call it our delight. . . . Nay, more, we even applied the torch to the work of our own hands, lest the sacred house should furnish shelter to our impious enemy. In a single day, and almost in a moment, we saw consumed our work of nearly ten years. . . . Desolated now is our home, desolated are our Penates. In the land of our exile we were forced to seek a new place of exile."

By November they had erected on the Island of St. Joseph a fort of solid masonry. It was one hundred feet square and fourteen feet high, and each corner was flanked by a bastion. In June some three hundred Hurons made their way to the island, most of them old people and widows with their children. Other groups arrived through the summer, and by fall the village numbered about a thousand. They had been living since March on acorns, roots, and what fish they could catch. "Seeing the Hurons," Father Chaumonot remarked, "you might conclude that they were dug-up corpses."

The French and Hurons eked out a miserable existence, weakened by hunger and reduced by influenza. The new year 1650 brought no new hope or better prospects, but emphasized their state of desperation. The Iroquois had found them out and could easily cross the channel, now frozen solid. "Our sleep," wrote Ragueneau, "was but half-sleep. Whatever the cold, whatever the snow, whatever winds might blow, sentinels kept watch all night long, exposed to every severity of weather in the never-ending rounds. The others who during this time were taking their periods of sleep were always under arms, as if awaiting the signal for battle."

Worse than the prowling Iroquois was the famine. The acorn supply was exhausted, and no more could be found under the snows on the island. In their extremity, the Hurons dug up the carrion of dogs, foxes, and other animals. As more of the people died, the survivors ate their corpses. "They even devoured one another," reports Ragueneau, "but this in secret, and with horror. No longer did necessity recognize any law. Famished teeth no more discerned the nature of what they ate. Mothers fed upon their children; children no longer recognized in a corpse him whom, while he lived, they had called their father."

In March a band crossing the ice in search of food drowned in sight of the fort. Other Hurons reached the mainland and were massacred by the Iroquois. In April parties went to their former fishing haunts and were slaughtered. From a survivor Ragueneau learned that two large Iroquois war parties were coming that summer to Huronia, one to level the villages, the other to wipe out the remnant on the Island of St. Joseph.

Two old chiefs pleaded with Ragueneau to lead the survivors to Quebec before they all perished, and their plea brought anguish to the missionaries; to comply would mean to abandon the far-west missions to the Hurons, Petuns, and Algonquins. Earnestly they prayed for guidance, and finally Ragueneau wrote the decision: "It seemed to us clearer and clearer that God spoke to us by the lips of these Huron chiefs. We ourselves saw that what they said was true. The entire Huron country was a land of horror and massacre. Everywhere we cast our eyes, we saw convincing proof that famine on the one hand and war on the other were completing the extermination of the few Christians who remained. If we were able to protect them as far as the shelter of the French fort at Montreal, Three Rivers, or Quebec, that would be their place of refuge."

Stephen Annaotaha, with a number of Huron warriors, was determined, however, to remain behind and to live and, if need be, to die in their own land. No bitterness or conflict arose between those who preferred to leave and those who elected to stay there. The Fathers and the other Frenchmen were unanimous in agreeing to the course suggested by the two chiefs, and by the end of May, they had built about sixty canoes to transport three hundred Hurons and fifty French to Quebec.

Once again they packed their few valuables, the most precious of which were the relics of Brébeuf, Gabriel Lalemant, and Garnier. Stephen and his scouts reported that the banks were free of Iroquois, and in dread silence on June 10, at nightfall, the Hurons and French stepped into their canoes and began their thousand-mile journey to Quebec.

As they moved away in the darkness from the second Sainte Marie they were obliged to abandon, Ragueneau's sad expression softened and his countenance lit up with bravery and with tenderness. In his hands he held the bones of Brébeuf, founder of the Huron mission. It was only twenty-four years ago, he reflected, that Jean had come to the Hurons, and only sixteen since he had won his first Huron to the Christian Faith. "During those sixteen years, observes Francis X. Talbot, "by the Providence of God, which none could understand and none could question, the Huron people and nations were brought to God and to death at the same time."[24]

As they had so frequently observed while on the missions, the outcome of all their work lay in the hands of God. They could

---

[24] Francis X. Talbot, *Saint Among the Hurons* (New York: Harper and Brothers, 1949), 320.

plant and they could water, but God alone could give the increase. They were content to do their best and to leave the issue in the hands of their Creator. "It was not without tears," wrote Ragueneau, "that we quitted the country that owned our hearts and held our hopes, which had already been reddened by the glorious blood of our brethren, which promised us a like happiness and which opened to us the road to Heaven and the gate of Paradise. *Mais quoy!* One must forget self and relinquish God's interests for God's sake."

Those Hurons who stayed on the Island of St. Joseph took possession of the stone fort. In the fall they repulsed a small band of Iroquois who crossed over to the island and attacked them. Soon after, a much larger war party approached undiscovered and built a fort opposite the island but hidden in the woods. Stephen Annaotaha and a few companions were caught in an ambush. They prepared hastily to defend themselves, but the Iroquois called out that they came not as enemies but as friends. They brought presents, they said, to persuade the Hurons to return with them as their adopted countrymen.

Stephen suspected treachery, but he concealed his suspicion and advanced with an air of perfect confidence. They pressed him to accept their invitation. Stephen, pointing out that there were among the Hurons older and wiser men than he, urged them to present their invitation to these and to keep him as a hostage. His apparent frankness disarmed them, and three of their leading chiefs agreed to do so, insisting that he accompany them. As they approached the fort, Stephen shouted the good news joyfully, and the Hurons expressed glee over the prospect held out to them. Then Stephen took aside a number of the Huron chiefs and confided to them his suspicion that the Iroquois were planning to destroy them under the cover of peace overtures. He proposed that they meet treachery with treachery, and it was agreed to execute his suggestion.

Now Stephen sent criers through the village who announced that all should prepare to migrate to the country of their new friends. Messages and visits were exchanged between Hurons and Iroquois, and the Iroquois were so confident that they sent thirty-seven of their best warriors to the Huron village. The time had come: at a signal from Stephen, the Hurons fell upon the Iroquois and cut them to pieces.

One Iroquois brave, just before he died, acknowledged that Stephen's suspicions were well founded; the Iroquois had indeed plotted to kill or capture all the Hurons.

A few minutes before the slaughter took place, Stephen had tipped off three of the Iroquois, so permitting them to escape. These were three who had enabled him to go free after he had been captured with Brébeuf and Lalemant in the mission of St. Louis, and in this way he discharged his debt of gratitude. To their countrymen on the mainland the three Iroquois carried news of the Huron vengeance. Aghast at the unexpected turn of events, all fled homeward in panic.

This victory sent a brief gleam of joy through the miseries of the Hurons, but it could not long hold back the tide that was to drive them forever from their homeland. Toward the end of winter, fearing retribution from the Iroquois, they fled across the frozen channel to Great Manitou Island. They remained there for a time, and then to the number of four hundred they descended the Ottawa River and rejoined the French and Hurons who had gone to Quebec the year before.

The united groups settled a short distance below Quebec, near the southwestern extremity of the Island of Orléans, on land belonging to the Jesuits. The Fathers had a fort built for the Hurons, and a little house and chapel for themselves. Around the ramparts of the fort the Hurons put up their bark cabins. They were provided with tools and seeds and were encouraged to cultivate the soil. The Indians gradually rallied from their dejected state, and the settlement commenced to thrive, but in 1656, their inveterate enemy attacked them and carried away a large number as captives.

The attenuated colony, augmented by straggling Hurons from other areas and still numbering several hundred persons, was removed to Quebec and lodged near the fort. They remained there for a decade, and when the danger had long since passed, they were transported to a place three or four miles west of Quebec, and subsequently to Old Lorette, nine miles from the fort. Here, under the guiding hand of Father Chaumonot, was erected a chapel in honor of Our Lady of Loretto, modeled after the Holy House of Loretto in Italy. The Faith blossomed there, and the examples of conspicuous virtue were many. Chaumonot reports that at the shrine of Our Lady, whither came pilgrims from many places, miraculous favors in great number were granted.

Shortly before the end of that century, the Hurons moved on to a place four miles distant, now called New Lorette, or Indian Lorette. It was in the primitive forest, where the St. Charles River foams over the black ledges and where the sunlight gleams through the pine and fir boughs. On a plateau beside the river, another chapel was erected to Our Lady, and a new Huron village sprang up.

Here the visitor finds the remnant of a lost people, harmless weavers of baskets and makers of moccasins. They have so generally intermarried with the French that no full-blooded Huron is among them. A nation, once powerful, for which many Jesuit missionaries labored and eight gave up their lives as martyrs, has vanished. The last curtain has fallen upon their people, but upon the memory of the gallant missionaries it can never fall.

~

Bibliography

The Jesuit Relations and Allied Documents. Edited by Reuben Gold Thwaites. 73 vols. Cleveland: The Burrows Company, 1896-1901. The biographies presented are based primarily upon data found in this masterly collection of original documents, an indispensable source for every student of the Jesuit missions in New France. We are grateful for permission to quote from it.

Talbot, Francis X. *Saint Among the Savages*. New York: Harper and Brothers, 1935; *Saint Among the Hurons*. New York: Harper and Brothers, 1949. These biographies of Jogues and Brébeuf are magnificent examples of historical scholarship. They embody all the important findings of modern research about the lives of these two missionaries and are the best one-volume biographies of them published in any language. They have been of great assistance in unraveling many parts of the tangled narrative in the *Relations* and are worthy of the highest praise.

Campbell, Thomas J. *Pioneer Priests of North America, 1642-1710*. 3 vols. New York: The America Press, 1908-1911.

These volumes present a splendid panorama of the vast Jesuit missionary enterprise in North America, along with detailed sketches and numerous illustrations. They are based upon the *Relations* and have proven of great practical help in preparing our book.

Parkman, Francis. *The Jesuits in North America in the Seventeenth Century*. Boston: Little, Brown and Company, 1867. This pioneer work has long been a classic. Written with a grandeur of diction and abounding in imagery and apt metaphor, it enchants the reader. Although it embodies the results of painstaking research, it is often impaired by the author's failure to appreciate the high spiritual motives and ideals of the missionaries.

~

Alegambe, Philippe, S. J. *Mortes Illustres, etc.* Brussels, 1655.

Archives of Collège Sainte-Marie, Montreal. Documents.

Autobiographie du P. Pierre Chaumont de la Compagnie de Jésus et son Complement. Traduite par P. Felix Martin, S.J. Paris, 1885.

Bancroft, George, *History of the United States*. Boston, 1850.

Becdelievre, Alain de, S.J. *Annales Religieuses du Diocese d'Orléans*. May 29, June 5, 1926. June 21, July 5, July 19, 1930.

Bennet, W. H. *Catholic Footsteps in Old New York*. New York, 1909.

Bracq, J. C. *The Evolution of French Canada*. New York, 1926.

Bressani, F. J. *Relation Abrégee de Quelques Missions des Pères de la Compagnie de Jésus*. Traduite par P. Félix Martin, S.J. Montreal, 1852.

Brodhead, John Romeyn. *History of the State of New York*. New York, 1853-1871.

Brodhead, John Romeyn, ed. *Documents Relative to the Colonial History of New York*. Vol. 1. Albany, 1856.

Brucker, Joseph, S.J. *La Compagnie de Jésus*. Paris, 1919.

Buteaux, Jacques. *The Capture of Father Jogues*. Translated in *Pilgrim of Our Lady of Martyrs*. New York: January-December, 1896.

Campbell, Thomas J., S.J. *The Jesuits, 1534-1921*. New York, 1921.

Casgrain, Abbé, H. R. *Histoire de l'Hôtel-Dieu de Quebec*. Quebec, 1878.

Catholic Encyclopedia. 16 vols. New York, 1913.

Catlin, George, *North American Indians*. 2 vols. London, 1841.

Creuxius, Franciscus, S.J. *Historiae Canadensis Libri Decem*. Paris, 1664.

Dionne, Narcisse E., *Samuel Champlain: Histoire de sa Vie et de ses Voyages*. 2 vols. Quebec, 1891.

Documents Relating to the Towns Along the Hudson and Mohawk Rivers. Edited by B. Fernow. Albany, 1881.

Ecclesiastical Records: State of New York, edited by Hugh Hastings. Albany, 1901.

Faillon, Abbé, *Histoire de la Colonie Française en Canada.*
3 vols. Montreal, 1865.

Ferland, J.B.A. *Cours d' Histoire du Canada.* Quebec,
1861.

Finley, John. *The French in the Heart of America.* New York,
1918.

Fouqueray, Henri, S.J., and Alain de Becdelievre, S.J.,
Martyrs du Canada. Paris, 1930.

—. *Histoire de la Compagnie de Jésus en France.* 5 vols.
Paris, 1922-1939.

Garneau, François-Xavier, *Histoire du Canada.* Paris, 1920.

Gosselin, Abbé A. *La Mission du Canada avant Mgr. de Laval:
Récollets et Jésuites.* Évreux, 1909.

Goyau, Georges, *Histoire religieuse de la nation françoise.*
Paris, 1922.

—. *Les origines religieuses du Canada.* Paris, 1924.

Hanotaux, Gabriel. *Histoire de la nation françoise.* 15 vols.
Paris, 1920-1924.

Hodge, F. W., ed. *Handbook of American Indians North of
Mexico.* Bulletin 30. Bureau of American Ethnology. 2
vols. Washington, D.C., 1907.

Innes, H. H. *New Amsterdam and Its People.* New York, 1902.

Jennes, Diamond, *The Indians of Canada.* Toronto, 1934.

Jones, Arthur E., S.J. *Old Huronia.* Toronto, 1909.

Travels and Sufferings of Father John de Brébeuf among the Hurons of Canada as Described by Himself. Translated from the French and Latin by Theodore Besterman. London, 1938.

Valentine, David. *History of the City of New York.* New York, 1853.

Weise, A. J. *History of the City of Albany.* Albany, 1884.

Works of Samuel de Champlain. Translated by H. H. Langton and W. F. Ganong. Edited by H. P. Biggar. Toronto, 1922-1936.

Wrong, George M., *The Rise and Fall of New France.* New York, 1928.

Wrong, George M. *Sagard's Long Journey to the Country of the Hurons.* Toronto, 1939.

Wynne, John J., S.J. *The Jesuit Martyrs of North America.* New York, 1925.

Lafitau, Joseph-François. *Moeurs des Sauvages Americains*. Paris, 1724.

Le Clercq, P. Christian. *First Establishment of the Faith in New France*. Translated by Shea. New York, 1881.

Les Annales de l'Hôtel Dieu de Quebec, 1636-1716. Composées par les RR. Mères Jeanne-Françoise Juchereau et Marie Andrée Duplessis. Editées par Dom Albert Jamet. Quebec, 1939.

Lescarbot, Marc, *The History of New France*. Translated by W. L. Grant. 3 vols. Toronto, 1907-1914.

Lettres de la Révérende Mère Marie de l'Incarnation. Editées par l'Abbé Richardeau. 3 vols. Tournai, 1876.

Marie de l'Incarnation: Écrits Spirituels et Historiques. Edited by Dom Albert Jamet. 4 vols. Paris and Quebec, 1929-1939.

Martin, Félix, S.J. *Le P. Isaac Jogues*. Paris and Quebec, 1874.

—. *The Life of Fr. Isaac Jogues*. Translated by Shea. New York, 1885.

—. *Hurons et Iroquois: le P. Jean de Brébeuf*. Paris, 1898.

Mélançon, Arthur, S.J. *Liste des Missionaires Jésuites*. Montreal, 1929.

Morgan, Lewis H. *League of the Iroquois*. 2 vols. New York, 1904.

O'Callaghan, E. B., ed. *Documentary History of the State of New York*, Vol. 4. Albany, 1851.

—. *History of New Netherlands*. 2 vols. New York, 1846.

Parkman, Francis, *Pioneers of France in the New World*. Boston, 1865.

Pilgrim of Our Lady of Martyrs. 1886 to date.

Pouliot, Léon, S.J. *Étude sur les Relations des Jésuites de la Nouvelle-France*. Montreal, 1940.

Première Mission des Jésuites au Canada, Lettres et Documents Inédits. Compiled by P. Auguste Carayon, S.J. Paris, 1864.

Rapport de l'Archiviste de la Province de Quebec pour 1924-1925. Edited by Pierre-Georges Roy. Quebec, 1925.

Reynolds, Cuyler, *Albany Chronicles*. Albany, 1906.

Richard, Edouard. *Acadie*. Édité par Henri d'Arles. 3 vols. Quebec, 1898-1903.

Rochemonteix, Camille de, S.J. *Les Jésuites de la Nouvelle-France*. Paris, 1895.

—. *Les Jésuites et la Nouvelle-France au XVII siècle d'après beaucoup de documents inédits*. Paris, 1895.

Roy, Pierre-Georges, *La Ville de Quebec sous le Régime Français*. 2 vols. Quebec, 1930.

Sagard-Theodat, Gabriel, Récollet. *Histoire du Canada et Voyages*. 4 vols. Paris, 1636.

—. *Le Grand Voyage du Pays des Hurons*. Paris, 1865.

Sulte, Benjamin, *Histoire des Canadiens-Français*. Montreal, 1882.

Tanner, Mathias, S.J. *Societas Jesu . . . Vita, et mors Eorum, etc.* Prague, 1675.

Sophia Institute Press®

Sophia Institute® is a nonprofit institution that seeks to restore man's knowledge of eternal truth, including man's knowledge of his own nature, his relation to other persons, and his relation to God. Sophia Institute Press® serves this end in numerous ways: it publishes translations of foreign works to make them accessible to English-speaking readers; it brings out-of-print books back into print; and it publishes important new books that fulfill the ideals of Sophia Institute®.

These books afford readers a rich source of the enduring wisdom of mankind. Sophia Institute Press® makes these high-quality books available to the general public by using advanced technology and by soliciting donations to subsidize its general publishing costs. Your generosity can help Sophia Institute Press® to provide the public with editions of works containing the enduring wisdom of the ages. Please send your tax-deductible contribution to the address below. We also welcome your questions, comments, and suggestions.

For your free catalog, call:
Toll-free: 1-800-888-9344

Sophia Institute Press® • Box 5284 • Manchester, NH 03108
www.sophiainstitute.com

Sophia Institute® is a tax-exempt institution as defined by the Internal Revenue Code, Section 501(c)(3). Tax I.D. 22-2548708.